The Book of Cricket Quotations

THE BOOK OF CRICKET QUOTATIONS

Peter Ball and David Hopps

Stanley Paul
London Melbourne Auckland Johannesburg

To the rheumatic hacks who have suffered years of working in primitive wooden press boxes, situated at square leg without a view of the scoreboard.

Copyright © Peter Ball and David Hopps 1986

All rights reserved

First published in 1986 by Stanley Paul & Co. Ltd,
Brookmount House, 62–65 Chandos Place, Covent Garden,
London WC2N 4NW

An imprint of Century Hutchinson Ltd

Century Hutchinson Australia (Pty) Ltd
PO Box 496, 16–22 Church Street, Hawthorn, Melbourne, Victoria 3122

Century Hutchinson New Zealand Limited
32-34 View Road, PO Box 40–086, Glenfield, Auckland 10

Century Hutchinson South Africa (Pty) Ltd
PO Box 337, Bergvlei 2012, South Africa

Set in Linotron Times in 10/11½ by
Input Typesetting Ltd, London SW19 8DR

Printed and bound in Great Britain by
R. J. Acford, Chichester, Sussex

British Library Cataloguing in Publication Data

Ball, Peter, *1943–*
    The book of cricket quotations.
    1. Cricket—Quotations, maxims, etc.
    I. Title II. Hopps, David
    796.35′8   PN6084.C7

ISBN 0 09 166151 X

Contents

Acknowledgements

Unlike football, Cricket has a huge literature; much of it literary in the worst, most arch way possible. Again unlike football, by and large cricket does not have an army of popular press journalists poised to snap up and record every word uttered by the main protagonists, the 1985/6 winter's tour of the West Indies of course excepted. And in the best English establishment traditions of secrecy, players' thoughts are carefully censored before they appear in print wherever possible by the TCCB and the counties. Because of this, the game's earthy realities are often captured less than adequately. We have tried to reflect these realities, so in the belief that the best sources of all are the journalists who know a good quote when they see one and can be relied upon to record it faithfully, our general thanks go to the 'hacks' who spent their days on the circuit. Without them this book would lack whatever immediacy it has.

To others we owe a more specific debt. Our thanks go to Tony Woodhouse for free access to his magnificent library of cricketana; to Phil Shaw, who chased up troublesome references in London clippings libraries; to Peter Cooper, Gerald Mortimer and Matthew Engel for their contributions; and to all the publishers and authors who waived copyright so magnanimously: especially *The Cricketer*, whose files proved a gold-mine.

Peter Ball
David Hopps

A Note on Sources

Wherever possible we have tried to be exact with our sources; at the same time we have wanted to avoid tedious repetition. To do so we have only repeated giving a source in full if we are using one person's quotes from a variety of sources in roughly equal proportions. We have relied heavily on *The Cricketer*, and unless they are otherwise identified, all quotes by C. I. (Buns) Thornton, Frank Mitchell, Gilbert Jessop, Sammy Woods, Archie MacLaren, Sir Pelham Warner and, in more modern times, Doug Insole and Peter Walker have been gleaned from their pages. Obviously quotes in the public domain – i.e. those widely reported in the press – are also not pinned down to a single source.

Photograph
Acknowledgements

The authors and publisher would like to thank the following for allowing the use of copyright photographs: All Sport, Associated Press, Colorsport, Patrick Eagar, The Mansell Collection, MCC, Eamonn McCabe and Sport and General Press Agency.

1
The Greats and Others

Players

G. O. Allen (Middlesex, England)

He does not get the best out of himself as a bowler, owing to
a somewhat rare temperament. For instance, instead of being
encouraged when a batsman plays at and just misses the ball, he
is the reverse. With a calmer serenity when bowling he might go
far.

PELHAM WARNER in *The Cricketer* on Allen's performances under him on the
MCC tour of South America, **1926/7**.

Benjamin Aislabie (MCC)

> But he still takes his bat, and there's no better fun
> Than to see him when batting attempting to run.

Rhyme on Benjamin Aislabie, overweight MCC secretary and reputedly one of
the worst batsmen to play at a high level, **1924**.

Bill Alley (Somerset, Australia)

Bill Alley will go down in cricket history for one unique, unrepeat-
able feat. Freddie Trueman once had to leave the Somerset
dressing room blushing modestly because the lurid language was
too much for him.

J. J. WARR, *The Cricketer*, **1962**.

Trevor Bailey (Essex, England)

Seeing Trevor Bailey prepare for a session in the field was like a lecture in anatomy.

RAY EAST, *A Funny Turn*, **1983**.

It requires an earthquake to make him change his game in midstream.

DOUG INSOLE, *Cricket From The Middle*, **1960**.

S. F. Barnes (Staffordshire, Lancashire, England)

If you wanted to score runs off Barnes, you had to score off good bowling.

LEARIE CONSTANTINE, after scoring 90 for Nelson v Rawtenstall when Barnes was 59.

At least if we go down, we'll take that bugger Barnes down with us.

A. C. MACLAREN during a rough trip home from Australia, **1902**. MacLaren had picked Barnes from League cricket to make the tour.

Ken Barrington (Surrey, England)

Whenever I see Ken coming to the wicket, I imagine the Union Jack fluttering behind him.

WALLY GROUT, **1965**.

Barrington was obviously not happy against the fast bowlers. Few batsmen are, but the majority hide their feelings. I think if I bowled to Barrington I should bowl a bouncer or two just to please my own ego, without having regard to the batsman's feelings.

W. E. BOWES on 2nd Test, England v S. Africa, **1960**.

Alec Bedser (Surrey, England)

Alec rolled his fingers over the ball as he delivered it, and as it swung it pitched on the seam and became, as it were, a leg-spinner. As it hit the turf, it would cut away sharply.

T. G. EVANS on Bedser's invention of the leg cutter.

Eric Bedser (Surrey)

Cor mate, your bloody hair grows quickly.

Sydney barber to Eric Bedser, entering the shop shortly after his twin brother, Alec, had left, **1950/51** tour.

William (Silver Billy) Beldham (Farnham, Surrey, 1780s)

Beldham was great in every hit, but his peculiar glory was the cut. Here he stood with no man beside him, the laurel was all his own; it was like the cut of a racket. His wrist seemed to turn on springs of the finest steel. He took the ball, as Burke did the House of Commons, between wind and water; not a moment too soon or too late.

REV. JOHN MITFORD, *The Gentleman's Magazine*, **1833**.

In his kitchen, black with age, but, like himself, still untouched by worms, hangs the trophy of his victories, the delight of his youth, the exercise of his manhood, and the glory of his age – his BAT.

REV. JOHN MITFORD on meeting Beldham, then 86 and living in Farnham.

Hon S. R. Beresford (Cambridge University)

A big slogger . . . who once hit Jessop out of Lord's; but he had the unfortunate habit of generally getting out too soon.

CROSS ARROW, *The Cricketer*, **1927**.

Jack Bond (Lancashire)

At 29 years of age, it seems that Bond is making a comparatively late bid to make his mark. In any case he has an assured future. He and his wife run a fish and chip shop.

LESLIE SMITH, *The Cricketer*, on Bond's 68 v Australians, **1961**.

David Boon (Australia)

Boon appears a most contented cricketer. I can visualise him on a sheep farm in Tasmania, sipping lager on the verandah, the ideal temperament for dealing with fast bowlers.

SIR LEN HUTTON, **1985**.

Allan Border (Essex, Australia)

Border has not so much a style as a *modus operandi*. He is utterly practical.

JOHN WOODCOCK, *The Times*, **1985**.

Ian Botham (Somerset, England)

He would probably not fit the bill as the schoolboy's vision of the dedicated superstar.

GRAHAM GOOCH, *Out Of The Wilderness*, **1985**.

I think if you made him Prime Minister tomorrow, he'd pick this country up in ten minutes.

BILL ALLEY, umpire, on Ian Botham, **1980**.

Ian Botham represents everything that's the best in Britain. He's Biggles, the VC, el Alamein, the tank commander, he's everything. I mean, how could a schoolboy not want to be like Ian Botham?

TIM HUDSON, Ian Botham's agent, **1985**.

Ian's so macho, man, when he looks at a girl it's like saying he's gonna rape her. He's got that look which says: 'It's your turn next' and the women love it. The Queen should knight him: Arise Sir Botham. That's his trip, man.

TIM HUDSON, **1985**.

He is to appear alongside Oliver Reed as a murderer and a rapist . . . he can't wait to get cracking.

The *Sun* on Botham's rumoured movie debut, **1985**.

In no way inhibited by any capacity to over-intellectualise. Repertoire of brilliantly witty party tricks includes pouring drinks down other players' girlfriends.

FRANCES EDMONDS, wife of England colleague Phil in *Daily Express*, **1985**.

He is the greatest match-winner the game has ever known.

MIKE BREARLEY, former England captain, **1985**.

He couldn't bowl a hoop downhill.

F. S. TRUEMAN, **1985**.

His role in the side is now clear; he is not a hack bowler to be allowed to bowl all day; he is a striker, to be taken off quickly if he looks below par, but allowed a fair degree of leeway to experiment. We should have more trust in his flair, and his instinct for wangling wickets.

MIKE BREARLEY replying to criticism of Botham's bowling in **1985**.

He must have put more backsides on seats than any other English cricketer since Denis Compton.

BOB TAYLOR, **1985**.

He couldn't bat to save himself. I bowled to him with a dicky arm during the 1977 tour and he was either dropped four times or made nought.

JEFF THOMSON, Australian paceman, **1980**.

He needs a father figure and I need a younger brother.

MIKE BREARLEY, speaking as a psycho-analyst about his relationship with Ian
Botham, during England's Test defeats of Australia, **1981**.

Anyone who dyes his hair that colour deserves to be caught on
the boundary.

Taunton old lady, about Ian Botham, **1985**.

So far as I know there has never been a St Ian. If ever one were
to be created, I can't think it would be anything to do with Ian
Terence Botham.

KATHY BOTHAM, after her husband confessed to smoking marijuana, **1986**.

Geoffrey Boycott (Yorkshire, England)

He is of the type who are likely to have enjoyed quite a fill of
wine, women and song.

FRASER WHITE, graphologist, analysing Geoffrey Boycott's handwriting in *The
Cricketer*, **1975**.

As I stood at the non-striker's end, I felt a wave of admiration
for my partner; wiry, slight, dedicated, a lonely man doing a lonely
job all these years. What is it that compels Geoffrey Boycott to
prove himself again and again among his peers?

MIKE BREARLEY, **1979**.

For a man with so much talent, I just feel it is sad that he is no
longer willing to offer it. The difficult thing to understand is how
any player can lose his appetite to play for his country.

MIKE DENNESS, England captain, on Geoffrey Boycott's self-imposed Test exile,
1975.

His ability to be where the fast bowlers aren't has long been a
talking point among cricketers.

TONY GREIG, after Boycott turned down Packer offer, **1978**.

The greatest tragedy of his troubled life is that, above all else, in the desire to be admired and loved by everyone, he has this enormous capacity for upsetting people.

TONY GREIG, **1983**.

I've been swamped by letters from ordinary Yorkshire members who can't contain their outrage. I've heard from others whose children won't stop crying because they'll never see Geoff bat again at Headingley.

SID FIELDEN, policeman, lay preacher and pro-Boycott organiser on Yorkshire committee, after the Yorkshire batsman's sacking, **1983**.

Geoffrey Boycott is a very great batsman. I wish I had never met him.

SID FIELDEN, formerly Boycott's greatest ally on the Yorkshire committee, in **1985**.

You have done for Australian cricket what the Boston strangler did for door-to-door salesmen.

JACK BIRNEY, Australian politician, to Boycott after grafting innings, England tour, **1978/79**.

The best slow batsman in the world.

KEITH FLETCHER, England captain, when Boycott left India tour early because of illness, **1982**.

Geoffrey Boycott is a giant playing among pygmies.

PETER BRIGGS, leader of Yorkshire Reform Group, **1981**.

Boycott for manager!

Section of Leeds United football crowd, dissatisfied with performances under Jimmy Adamson, **1980**.

I had a wonderful letter from Boycott saying that it was entirely due to me that he was a good cricketer.

BARBARA CARTLAND, *Daily Mail*, **1981**.

On only 45 occasions, I estimate, did Boycott give Essex the
slightest hope. Just before lunch he played and missed at Boyce;
at 84 he popped a ball which had checked just short of cover;
there was one appeal for lbw that might not have been too far
away, and on 42 occasions he might have been run out.

ALAN GIBSON, *The Times*, on Boycott's double century for Yorkshire v Essex,
1971.

Boycott and I are different. He's not so much a role model as an
inspiration.

TIM ROBINSON, England opening batsman, **1985**.

There was a certain gentleman from Yorkshire out there who
managed to find some practice facilities.

RAY ILLINGWORTH, **1986**. Boycott's search for net facilities had been rather more
successful than England's during the West Indies Test series.

Sir Don Bradman (Australia)

There's no ruddy best ball to bowl at The Don.

BILL VOCE, **1933**.

Bradman was a team in himself. I think the Don was too good:
he spoilt the game. He got too many runs. The pot calling the
kettle black? No, I was human; he got hundreds every time he
went in . . . He was mechanical; he was the greatest run-getting
machine of all time. I do not think we want to see another one
quite like him. I do not think we ever shall.

JACK HOBBS, *The Times*, **1952**.

Few will be found to admit that the hero-worship, almost
amounting to idolatry, to which, for example, Bradman was
subject, is desirable for the game's good.

DOUGLAS JARDINE, **1933**.

No-one ever laughed about Bradman. He was no laughing matter.

R. C. ROBERTSON-GLASGOW.

Bradman was the summing up of the Efficient Age which succeeded the Golden Age. Here was brilliance safe and sure, streamlined and without impulse. Victor Trumper was the flying bird; Bradman the aeroplane.

NEVILLE CARDUS, *Autobiography*, **1947**.

Each slow mouthful was an essay in methods of digestion, in relaxation, in cold planning and contemplation of the real feast ahead.

JACK FINGLETON on Bradman's lunch-hour eating manner.

Bradman fails again.

English newspaper placard, winter of **1936** (he had narrowly missed a century).

William Clarke (Founder of the All England XI)

Excepting his own faults, Clarke knew more than any man alive about cricket.

GEORGE PARR (quoted in E. W. Swanton's revision of H. S. Altham, *A History of Cricket*). **1962**

Brian Close (Yorkshire, Somerset, England)

In future, I shall always be able to tell when the cricket season begins. All I have to do is listen for the sound of Brian Close being hit by a cricket ball.

ERIC MORECAMBE, comedian, after Close withstood West Indian bumper barrage on return to Test cricket, **1976**.

Denis Compton (Middlesex, England)

I wouldn't say I coached him, but I didn't mess him up.

GEORGE FENNER, head coach at Lord's, on his early coaching of Compton, **1958**.

He was the only player to call his partner for a run and wish him good luck at the same time.

JOHN WARR, his Middlesex colleague, in *The Cricketer*.

If my mother hadn't thrown my football boots on the fire, I might have become as famous as Denis Compton.

LEN HUTTON.

Learie Constantine (West Indies)

He revolted against the revolting contrast between his first-class status as a cricketer and his third-class status as a man.

C. L. R. JAMES, *Beyond A Boundary*, **1963.**

Mike Denness (Kent, Essex, England)

To dismiss this lad Denness you don't have to bowl fast. You just have to run up fast.

BRIAN CLOSE, **1974.**

Peter Denning (Somerset)

If he worried about all the things he can't do, he'd never score a run.

PETER ROEBUCK, Somerset batsman, in *It Never Rains*, **1984.**

Ted Dexter (Sussex, England)

Errol Holmes is called 'the last of the dandies' – yet Dexter is seen as a possible successor. Does a dandy chew gum? Who knows – nowadays?

G. D. MARTINEAU, *The Cricketer*.

Graham Dilley (Kent, England)

Cowans should remember what happened to Graham Dilley, who started off as a genuinely quick bowler. Then they started stuffing 'line and length' into his ear, and now he has Dennis Lillee's action with Denis Thatcher's pace.

GEOFFREY BOYCOTT, **1982.**

J. W. H. T. Douglas (Essex, England)

The only thing that seems to upset him is when he has beaten the batsman and just missed the wicket. On such occasions he is apt to throw his arms about.

The Cricketer 'Portrait of Douglas', **1921**.

He has earned great fame as a boxer, and in the ring his quickness of foot is exceptional; but at cricket his boots always seem too big for him and too heavy.

The Cricketer 'Portrait of Douglas', **1921**.

Ray East (Essex)

His epitaph will be the stories he created, stories which became bar room legends around the cricket circuit. Cricketers swap Ray East experiences rather as some people swap Irish jokes.

GRAHAM GOOCH, East's Essex colleague, in *Out Of The Wilderness*, **1985**.

Phil Edmonds (Middlesex, England)

Reputation for being arrogant and awkward, probably because he is arrogant and awkward. Works very hard at trying to be controversial and iconoclastic, but basically a pillar of the establishment.

FRANCES EDMONDS, *Daily Express*, **1985**.

Phil Edmonds needs two more field changes to get his 1,000 for the season.

JIM LAKER, **1985**.

John Emburey (Middlesex, England)

I could never be a 100 per cent professional like John Emburey.

PHIL EDMONDS, his Middlesex and England spin colleague, **1982**.

He's come a long way from Peckham, particularly after marriage
to his second wife, Australian Sue.

FRANCES EDMONDS, *Daily Express*, **1985**.

I'm not a flighty bowler. I like to use my control to put pressure
on the batsman, react to what he does and force him into error.
And my bowling doesn't really change. So I'm not so good at
exploiting a bad wicket; I'm a hard wicket bowler.

JOHN EMBUREY.

A conversation with him would be 50 per cent shorter if he deleted
the expletives.

MIKE SELVEY, **1985**.

Tom Emmett (Yorkshire, 1870s/80s)

He frequently bowled wides, but frequently also an unplayable
ball even on the best of wickets. With an odd, angular sort of
delivery, he was in his early days very fast, and on the old-
fashioned wickets very dangerous . . . As a batsman he had some
of the same characteristics that he had as a bowler in his complete
disregard of the conventional. Originally mainly a hitter, he
became later on quite a steady player – but nobody could prophesy
what he was going to do. A half-volley that nine batsmen out of
ten would hit to the ropes Emmett would play gently back to the
bowler, while a good-length ball he would jump out at and hit for
four.

Obituary, *The Times*, **1904**.

Felix (Nicholas Wanostrocht) (Kent, 1840s)

He knew the whole science of the game, and had a hand and eye
such as no one e'er beat him at; and when he saw the ball was
pretty well safe to keep outside the off-stump, it was a beautiful
thing to see him throw his right foot forward – he was left-handed
– and do a little, bit of tip-toeing with his bat over his shoulder.

FULLER PILCH, quoted in H. S. Altham and E. W. Swanton's *A History of
Cricket*. **1962**

C. B. Fry (Surrey, Sussex, Hampshire)

He was one of the last of his kind – and certainly the finest specimen of it – the amateurs, the smiling gentlemen of games, intensely devoted to the skill and the struggle but always with a certain gaiety, romantic at heart but classical in style.

J. B. PRIESTLEY, *The English*, 1973.

Joel Garner (Somerset, West Indies)

Blimey, the bugger can't bend as well can he?

BRIAN CLOSE, 1977.

They should cut him off at the knees to make him bowl at a normal height.

GEOFFREY BOYCOTT, during England's tour of Caribbean, 1981.

David Gower (Leicestershire, England)

Difficult to be more laid back without being actually comatose.

FRANCES EDMONDS, *Daily Express*, 1985.

If Gower were an Aussie, he'd be in my team every time.

ALLAN BORDER, Australian captain, on criticisms of Gower's poor form in the first months of 1985.

Gower is world class and was going through a bad patch. We all do. The backslapping David is getting now does not make up for the cruel taunts he had to endure.

ALLAN BORDER on Gower's transformation from villain to hero in 1985.

Perhaps Gower will eventually realise cricket's not always about champagne. It's a bread and butter game.

BRIAN BRAIN, Gloucestershire seamer, *Another Day, Another Match*, 1981.

E. M. Grace (Gloucestershire, England)

The stir that EM made was all the greater because of the scandalous manner in which he outraged every law of batting that had hitherto been held sacred.

BERNARD DARWIN, *W. G. Grace*, **1934**.

Earliest, and not least famous of Cowshotters.

A. C. M. CROOME.

'Uncle Ted's' proximity to the batsman, apart from the chances of a catch, was no inconceivable asset to the bowler. He kept up a running commentary with the batsman, which, in the case of some, was apt to prevent that entire concentration of thought which is so requisite for success.

G. L. JESSOP, in *The Cricketer*. Uncle Ted was Grace the elder's nickname.

One of the old school, if words could not settle the argument to his entire satisfaction, he liked nothing better than a suggestion from an opponent that tongues were not the only weapons of settlement. Often the suggestion came first from himself.

G. L. JESSOP, *The Cricketer*.

E. M. Grace and his brothers (Gloucestershire, England)

The 'three Graces' played for England; they were a remarkable trio, dark, hard, active, hirsute men – E. M. Grace, the (original) 'Doctor', always very noisy. W.G., very determined as to what he conceived to be the rights of his side, and occasionally excitable, but, as a rule, calmly contemplative of the fortunes of the game; G.F., of a much softer temperament, most amiable and genial.

LORD HARRIS on the **1880** England v Australia Test at The Oval.

W. G. Grace (Gloucestershire, England)

He revolutionized cricket. He turned it from an accomplishment into a science.

RANJITSINHJI, *The Jubilee Book of Cricket*, **1897**.

What W.G. did was to unite in his mighty self all the good points of all the good players, and to make utility the criterion of style.

RANJITSINHJI, *The Jubilee Book of Cricket*, **1897**.

He turned the old one-stringed instrument into a many chorded lyre. But in addition he made his execution equal his invention.

RANJITSINHJI, *The Jubilee Book of Cricket*, **1897**.

W.G.'s name will not be associated with any one stroke because, when he was physically in his prime, he played them all at least as well as the specialists. Even when he was fat and heavy-footed he made a thousand runs in May largely by pulling the ball powerfully and for longer periods than his brother E.M. ever could.

A. C. M. CROOME.

Admission 3d; If Dr. W. G. Grace plays, Admission 6d.

Notice outside grounds in 1870s.

I call him a nonsuch; he ought to be made to play with a littler bat.

TOM EMMETT, of Yorkshire, after W. G. Grace hit a century for South v North at Sheffield, quoted in Lord Hawke's *Recollections and Reminiscences*, **1922**.

It's Grace before meat, Grace after dinner and Grace all the time.

TOM EMMETT.

The first ball I sent whizzing through his whiskers; after that he kept hitting me off his blinkin' ear 'ole for 4.

ERNEST JONES, Australia, on game v Lord Sheffield's XI, **1896**.

It ain't a bit of use my bowling good 'uns to him now; it's a case of I puts the ball where I please and he puts it where he pleases.

JEMMY SHAW, Notts' fast bowler, brought on when W. G. Grace was well set, **1870s**.

What, are you going, Doctor? There's still one stump standing.

CHARLES KORTRIGHT, Essex pace bowler, to W. G. Grace after bowling him.

One of the dirtiest necks I ever kept wicket behind.

LORD COBHAM, on W. G. Grace.

Tom Graveney (Gloucestershire, Worcestershire, England)

He played for Gloucestershire, he works for us.

LEN COLDWELL, Worcestershire team-mate, on Tom Graveney's change of attitude, **1966**.

David Green (Lancashire, Gloucestershire)

If ever there was a larger-than-life guy, it was Greeny; extremely intelligent and witty, he had an old-fashioned attitude to new-fangled things such as training and fitness programmes. He didn't believe in them. For him, cricket was a way of making a lot of friends, knocking the cover off the ball if possible and making regular attempts to boost the profits of certain breweries.

MIKE PROCTER, in *Mike Procter and Cricket*, **1981**.

Jack Gregory (Australia)

It is no secret, at any rate with spectators, that Mr J. M. Gregory, by reason of the shortness of his length, is suspect of being indifferent as to the safety of opposing batsmen.

G. L. JESSOP.

Clarrie Grimmett (Australia)

Clarrie was responsible, self-disciplined, considerate and studious. This man thought a full toss was the worst form of cricket vandalism and the long hop a legacy from prehistoric days when barbarians rolled boulders towards the enemy.

ARTHUR MAILEY, *10 for 66 and All That*. **1958**

One of the gentlest of bowlers ever to lift a ball, he walked gently, picked up a cup of tea gently, arranged his tie with whispering fingers. His cap was set as though with a spirit level – none of this Yorkshire tilt for the fastidious Mr Grimmett.

ARTHUR MAILEY, *10 for 66 and All That*. **1958**

Wally Grout (Australia)

If you threw a ball to Wally Grout a bit off target you'd get the full treatment. One hell of a glare and something like: 'These hands are my life, protect them!'

NEIL HAWKE, **1972**.

William Gunn (Nottinghamshire)

I felt tired of cricket perhaps once – when I listened to Billy Gunn saying 'No!' at Lord's for seven and a half hours.

SYDNEY GREGORY on Gunn's 228 for Players v Australia, Lord's **1890**.

Louis Hall (Yorkshire, 1880s)

I'd be glad to pay for the coffin in which to bury this tyke.

HUMPHREYS, Sussex lob bowler, frustrated by Yorkshire's Louis Hall ('Old Stolidity'), **1883**, quoted by Lord Hawke.

Wes Hall (West Indies)

It was the first time two batsmen have ever crossed in the toilet.

TONY LEWIS, facing Wes Hall, the West Indian pace bowler, for the first time, Glamorgan v West Indies, **1963**.

Wally Hammond (Gloucestershire, England)

We Australians heard that Wally Hammond was very weak on the legside, that he was solely an offside batsman. Very well, we bowled outside the leg to keep him quiet or tease him into doing something desperate. Clarrie Grimmett, the arch conspirator, with sinister intent at Adelaide pegged away a foot or two outside Wally's leg-stump waiting patiently for the great batsman to make a wild, uncharacteristic swing and be caught in front of the ladies' stand. Nothing happened. The ladies went on knitting or shelling peas for hubby's dinner.

ARTHUR MAILEY.

Clarrie, with that fastidious judgement few bowlers possess, sent down a ball in line with leg-stump. Almost simultaneously the ball crashed into the cover fence under the scoreboard.

ARTHUR MAILEY.

Brian Hardie (Essex)

Hardie's knock made some of Trevor Bailey's stuff look quick.

KEITH FLETCHER, Essex captain, after Brian Hardie scored four singles in 142 minutes, slowest championship innings, v Hampshire at Chelmsford, **1974**.

David Harris (Hambledon, All England)

His attitude, when preparing to deliver the ball, was masculine, erect and appalling. First he stood like a soldier at drill, upright. Then with a graceful and elegant curve, he raised the fatal ball to his forehead, and drawing back his right foot, started off. Woe be to the unlucky Wight who did not know how to stop these cannonades! His fingers would be ground to dust against the bat, his bones pulverised, and his blood scattered over the field . . . Harris was terribly afflicted with the gout; it was at length difficult for him to stand, a great armchair was always brought into the field, and after the delivery of the ball, the hero sat down in his own calm and simple grandeur, and reposed.

REV. JOHN MITFORD on David Harris, Hambledon's fast bowler, *Gentleman's Magazine*, **1833**.

Tom Hayward (Surrey)

(He) was my greatest bugbear. He was what may be called a 'flat-catching' bowler. He looked so much simpler than he really was. Over confidence rather than diffidence of my ability to cope with him usually upset my applecart, for I could never rid myself of the conviction that in almost every ball there lurked a half-volley.

G. L. JESSOP.

Major Henshaw (Wiltshire, 1920s)

Major Henshaw, who stands well over six feet, can send down a nasty ball on occasion, especially if the sight screen is low.

R. O. EDWARDS in *The Cricketer* on Wiltshire's prospects for 1921.

George Hirst (Yorkshire, England)

How the devil can you play a ball that comes at you like a hard throw-in from cover-point?

S. M. J. WOODS on Hirst's bowling.

I have tossed my slow tripe at you till I grew weary, and I longed for the shades of eve. There was no man I would rather have made 50 off than you; no man I was more pleased to get out.

D. L. A. JEPHSON ('the Lob-ster') tribute on Hirst's 50th birthday.

Sir Jack Hobbs (Surrey, England)

It were impossible to fault him. He got 'em on good 'uns, he got 'em on bad 'uns, he got 'em on sticky 'uns, he got 'em on t'mat, against South African googlers, and he got 'em all over t'world.

WILFRED RHODES.

Michael Holding (Lancashire, Derbyshire, West Indies)

A perfect running specimen, but I don't go to a Test to see running; if I wished to see that I would go to Crystal Palace to see Coe and Ovett.

JACK FINGLETON in *Batting From Memory*. **1981**

Percy Holmes (Yorkshire)

It is worth padding many miles with a nail in your boots to see him in the field.

R. O. EDWARDS in *The Cricketer*, **1921**.

A. N. (Monkey) Hornby (Lancashire, England, 1880s)

First he runs you out of breath, then he runs you out; and then he gives you a sovereign.

RICHARD BARLOW (Lancashire professional) on his amateur opening partner.

After leaving Harrow . . . he went up to Oxford with the sole intention of 'playing cricket' (as he said), but, on being informed that he would have to undertake certain lessons, and having no liking for books, he made rather a hurried departure.

W. E. HOWARD, *50 Years' Cricket Reminiscences*, **1928**.

Davy Hunter (Yorkshire, 1890s)

He was almost apologetic when he secured you as a victim. He made you feel that if the matter was left entirely in his hands – well, you could continue your rudely interrupted innings.

G. L. JESSOP, *The Cricketer*, on the Yorkshire wicket-keeper.

Sir Len Hutton (Yorkshire, England)

I am only setting up these records for Hutton to break them.

HERBERT SUTCLIFFE, Yorkshire batsman.

There's nothing we can teach this lad.

GEORGE HIRST, Yorkshire coach, on Hutton's first appearance at county nets, **1930**.

Hutton was never dull. His bat was part of his nervous system. His play was sculptured. His forward defensive stroke was a complete statement.

HAROLD PINTER, *Cricket '72*, **1972**.

Sir F. S. Jackson (Yorkshire, England)

As I looked down on that vast congregation of cricketers who had known him, I could see from the rapt expression on their faces how they felt towards the great man . . . how they revered him; how indeed they reverenced him as though he were the Almighty, but infinitely stronger on the leg side.

Ascribed by George Cox to the bishop delivering Jackson's funeral oration.

Kevin Jarvis (Kent)

If I could bowl at myself, I would be very keen. It would be an amputation job to get the ball out of my hands.

KEVIN JARVIS, who averaged 3·15 with the bat in **1985**, after preventing Agnew claiming all ten wickets.

G. L. Jessop (Gloucestershire, England)

Jessop was a terror. We reckoned in this game we'd make him go and fetch 'em. So we bowled wide on the offside. He fetched 'em all right. He went off like a spring-trap and, before you'd seen his feet move, he was standing on the offside of his stumps, pulling 'em over the square-leg boundary.

WILFRED RHODES on Jessop's century in each innings for Gloucestershire against Yorkshire, **1900** (quoted by A. A. Thomson, *Hirst and Rhodes*).

His speed of foot and eye and judgement, his strength of wrist, his timing and daring, all made him the most dangerous batsman the world will ever see; he didn't go in for huge hits; he made boundaries out of balls that the best batsmen would be content just to play.

s. m. j. woods, *The Cricketer.*

Charles Kellaway (Australia)

Kellaway will be a great cricketer some day – in the next world, where time will be of no account.

CECIL PARKIN after Kellaway took 7 hours over 147 v England, Adelaide, **1927**.

Jim Laker (Surrey, England)

Macartney or Woolley would have killed Laker. And without referring to my *Wisden* I could name twenty more batsmen who would have driven the good-looking off-breaker into the dust.

ARTHUR MAILEY on Laker's 19 wickets for 90 runs v Australia, Old Trafford, **1956**.

No bugger ever got all 10 when I was at the other end.

SYDNEY BARNES, after watching Jim Laker take all 10 wickets for England v Australia, Old Trafford, **1956**.

Dennis Lillee (and Jeff Thomson, Australia)

Ashes to ashes, dust to dust – If Thomson don't get ya, Lillee must . . .

Sydney Telegraph cartoon caption, **1975**.

There's no batsman on earth who goes out to meet Dennis Lillee and Jeff Thomson with a smile on his face.

CLIVE LLOYD, **1975**.

I don't really like the new Dennis Lillee. There's no substitute for bowling fast and being able to make the good players jump.

DENNIS LILLEE, *My Life in Cricket*, **1982**.

A great fast bowler, the best I have ever seen and one of the finest of all time. He had everything: courage, variety, high morale, arrogance, supreme fitness and aggression . . . but I am afraid I will also remember him as the bloke who stopped playing for love of the game and his country and started playing for money and to please the TV producers.

BOB WILLIS, *The Cricket Revolution*, **1981**.

Dick Lilley (Kent, England, 1890s)

In all the time I watched him, I never saw him on his backside.

E. J. 'TIGER' SMITH on his fellow wicket-keeper.

Ray Lindwall (Australia)

He was a great man at a party, and played his part in ensuring that no English brewery went out of business through lack of patronage.

JIM LAKER, *Over to Me*. **1960**

George Macaulay (Yorkshire, 1920s)

There's only one man made more appeals than you, George, and that was Dr Barnardo.

BILL REEVE, umpire.

Jack MacBryan (Somerset, 1920s)

That one looks more like a Yorkshire professional than a Somerset amateur.

WILFRED RHODES, on watching MacBryan bat for MCC v Yorkshire at Scarborough.

Stan McCabe (Australia)

Come and see this. Don't miss a minute of it. You'll never see
the likes of this again.

DON BRADMAN to Australian side during Stan McCabe's 232 v England at Trent
Bridge, **1938**.

Ken Mackay (Australia)

The derisive roar of laughter which greeted his famous goalkeeper
shot against Laker still burns in my ears.

ARTHUR MAILEY.

Despite the apparent visual evidence of his batting to the contrary,
Mackay is a natural ball-games player.

JOHN ARLOTT, *The Cricketer*, **1963**.

He is the only athlete I have ever known who, as he walked,
sagged at ankles, knees and hips.

JOHN ARLOTT, *The Cricketer*, **1963**.

Arthur Mailey (Australia)

If Arthur Mailey was not cricket's greatest bowler, he was its
greatest philosopher.

BEN TRAVERS, **1967**.

Philip Mead (Hampshire, England)

I wonder if there has been another player who understood the
science of batsmanship as much as Mead.

HERBERT SUTCLIFFE.

Mead, you've been in five hours and you've just stonewalled.

R. W. V. ROBINS to Mead, when he had made 218 not out in five hours v Middlesex.

Mead – get on or get out – signed Tennyson.

Telegram delivered to Philip Mead, Hampshire batsman, during slow innings at
Lord's, from his captain Lord Tennyson, mid-**1920s**.

Hello, Mead, I saw your father play in 1911.

Australian, mistakenly, to Mead, who toured Australia with MCC in 1911 and
1928.

Colin Milburn (Northamptonshire, England)

He is as untidy as an unmade bed, as devastating as a hand
grenade.

CLIVE TAYLOR, the *Sun*, **1968**.

I've always been a slogger and my father was a slogger before
me.

COLIN MILBURN, **1966**.

Arthur Mold (Lancashire, 1880s)

Personally Mold was the nicest of men, and I am certain he never
intentionally threw.

PELHAM WARNER. Mold bowled fast off six paces, and was no-balled 16 times in
10 overs for throwing against Somerset at Old Trafford.

Alfred Mynn (Kent, 1840s)

With his tall and stately presence, with his nobly moulded
form,
His broad hand was ever open, his brave heart was ever
warm,
All were proud of him, all loved him. As the changing
seasons pass,
As our champion lies a-sleeping underneath the Kentish
grass,
Proudly, sadly will we name him – to forget him were a sin.
Lightly lie the turf upon thee, kind and manly Alfred
Mynn!

WILLIAM JEFFREY PROWSE, In Memoriam, Alfred Mynn, last verse.

Chris Old (Yorkshire, Warwickshire, England)

Fit and bowling well, he's a very fine player. I just wish he had more heart.

RAY ILLINGWORTH, *Yorkshire and Back*, **1980**.

Bill O'Reilly (Australia)

When bowling, he completely dominated the situation. He roared at umpires and scowled at batsmen. There was no sign of veneer or camouflage when he appealed, nor were there any apologies or beg pardons when the umpire indicated that the batsmen's legs were yards out of line with the stumps.

ARTHUR MAILEY.

To hit him for four would usually arouse a belligerent ferocity which made you sorry. It was almost like disturbing a hive of bees. He seemed to attack from all directions.

SIR DON BRADMAN, *Farewell To Cricket*, **1950**.

Who is this man with creaking bones,
This ancient uttering oaths and groans,
Bowling roundarms, and that most vilely?
Sir, 'tis the ghost of Bill O'Reilly.

SIR ROBERT MENZIES, Australian prime minister, celebrating O'Reilly's appearance in his eleven, Canberra, **1952**.

His googly was harder to spot than a soda-fountain in the bush.

COLIN MCCOOL, *Cricket Is A Game*, **1961**.

Cecil Parkin (Lancashire, England)

He took 14 wickets in the match. He bowled every possible variety of ball from fast-medium away swingers to the highest of full-tosses; he swung it both ways, he spun like a top, producing out of the hat leg-break, off-break, top-spinner and googly, with an occasional straight ball for good measure.

C. S. MARRIOTT on Parkin's 14 wickets v Yorkshire in *The Complete Leg-Break Bowler*.

Had it been possible, he would have bowled more than six different balls per over. In his continual startling variations of pace he actually gave the illusion, at the end of one over, of having brought his right hand over empty and served up a lob with his left. In another, he played the farcical trick when he suddenly stopped dead three yards behind the bowling crease and delivered a high, slow donkey-drop which, of all people, foxed out George Hirst.

C. S. MARRIOTT.

George Parr (Nottinghamshire, 1840s)

There is a tree at Nottingham which is, or was, known as George Parr's tree. It was situated at square leg, and it was his particular delight to hit over this bramble. All I can say is that the bowlers who gave him this particular ball were silly asses; no one supposed to be a bowler had any right to indulge the said veteran.

SAMMY WOODS.

Ted Peate (Yorkshire, England, 1880s)

One of my saddest tasks was to dismiss him from the Yorkshire eleven. But he bore me no grudge, and whenever I subsequently ran across him, invariably he greeted me with the old familiar smile and the same slow, spontaneous: 'Good morning, my Lord, I hope you are as well as I am.'

LORD HAWKE.

Bobby Peel (Yorkshire, England, 1890s)

He seemed to push the ball up to one as if he was leisurely putting the weight. Half-volleys from him you had to fetch, and it was in the fetching that Bobby reaped such a rare harvest.

G. L. JESSOP.

Fuller Pilch (Kent, 1830s)

I wish I had as many pounds as I have bowled Pilch.

WILLIAM LILLYWHITE.

They may call it Pilch's 'poke' if they please, but I rather fancy that Pilch's 'poke' would puzzle some of our present-day bowlers. If a 'poke' means smothering the ball before it has time to rise and break, and placing it to the off or on with the greatest apparent ease, I shall much like to see it done again in these days.

FRED GALE, *The Game of Cricket*, 1870.

Mike Procter (Gloucestershire, South Africa)

The amazing thing about Procter is that he goes out with any bat he picks up; he never worries about the weight, balance or pick-up of a bat; he just goes out there and hammers it.

BRIAN BRAIN, 1979.

Sonny Ramadhin (West Indies)

Like trying to play a boonch of confetti.

Ascribed to a Derbyshire batsman by IAN PEEBLES, *Batter's Castle*. 1958

All you see is a blur of black hand, a white shirt with sleeves buttoned down to the wrist and a red blur.

DENIS COMPTON's advice to Keith Miller, on Ramadhin, 1951.

Derek Randall (Nottinghamshire, England)

He is the oddest mixture of uncertainty and hectic over-confidence. Somewhere between the two, and especially when his side is in peril, he is a balanced, shrewd, player; a natural batsman whose judgement is reliable; his defence sound; his strokes flowingly appropriate to the ball bowled.

JOHN ARLOTT, 1983.

Ranjitsinhji (Sussex, England, 1900s)

The coming of Ranji rather upset the 'off theory' business.

G. L. JESSOP.

He did not wait for the ball off the wicket from which to perform his leg-glide stunt, but persisted in persuading the straight ball to take the onside course.

G. L. JESSOP.

After being warned for years of the danger of playing back on a fast wicket, and especially to fast bowling, it came as rather a surprise to see the great Indian batsman transgressing against a principle so firmly fixed in one's mind.

G. L. JESSOP.

To attribute the two-shouldered stance to his wonderful leg-glides is absurd. To begin with he did not put his left leg on the on-side, as so many modern players do in attempting this stroke, but placed his left leg across his right leg on the off-side of the wicket, and at the same time deflected the ball with the turn of his wrists at the moment of impact.

SIR PELHAM WARNER, *The Cricketer*, 1923.

He's no batsman, he's a conjuror.

GEORGE GIFFEN, Australian.

Sam Redgate (Nottinghamshire)

His weakness was well known, and there was a general conspiracy to pass the tankard.

FELIX, on the method employed against a feared fast bowler.

Ian Redpath (Australia)

He is everything most Australians are not . . . a model of batting technique.

RAY ILLINGWORTH, 1972.

Wilfred Rhodes (Yorkshire, England)

Was there any ball that Hedley Verity bowled that you didn't
bowl yourself?
Yes, there was the ball that they cut for four.

Exchange between questioner and Wilfred Rhodes.

When George (Hirst) got you out, you were out. When Wilfred
got you out, you were out twice, because he knew by then how
to get you out in the second innings too.

ROY KILNER, Yorkshire team-mate.

Wilfred studied the game more than a financier ever studied the
stock market.

BILL BOWES, *Express Deliveries*, 1949.

Wilfred couldn't see the stumps at my end. I could have been no
more than a blurred and distant image, yet, bowling from
memory, with his arm upright, he flighted the ball beautifully and
dropped on a good length six times out of six. I played through
a maiden over on merit and was glad enough to survive it.

BRIAN SELLARS, describing Wilfred Rhodes's near-blind opening over to open a
new ground near Wakefield at the age of 72, **1949**.

. R. C. Robertson-Glasgow (Somerset, 1920s)

The best bowler this year . . . but his services should not be relied
on to any great extent as he never seems to rise to the occasion.
In the 3 years that he has represented Oxford at Lord's, he has
only captured 1 wicket.

'Isis' in *The Cricketer*, **1923**, on Oxford's prospects in the Varsity match.

If I had my way, you wouldn't bat at all.

JOHN DANIELL, Somerset captain, in reply to Robertson-Glasgow's asking his
place in the batting order.

Emmott Robinson (Yorkshire)

Robinson seemed to be made out of the stuff of Yorkshire county; I imagine that the Lord one day gathered together a heap of Yorkshire clay and breathed into it and said, 'Emmott Robinson, go and bowl at the pavilion end for Yorkshire.'

NEVILLE CARDUS, *Good Days*. The amended version in Cardus's autobiography gives God a Yorkshire accent instead of Yorkshire clay.

Peter Roebuck (Somerset)

Watching Roebuck was like being at a Requiem Mass.

JIM LAKER after Roebuck scored 34, including 2 fours, in 2hrs 43 minutes v Surrey, **1985**. Roebuck had previously criticised Laker's 'dirge-like' commentating.

Peter Sainsbury (Hampshire)

I'm all right when his arm comes over but I'm out of form by the time the bloody ball gets here.

FRED TRUEMAN, describing his problems against Sainsbury, **1963**.

W. Scotton (Nottinghamshire, England, 1880s)

Block, block, block,
At the foot of thy wickets, ah do!
But one hour of Grace or Walter Read
Were worth a week of you!

Punch after Scotton had scored 34 in 3¾ hours v Australia, Oval, **1886**.

Arthur Shrewsbury (Nottinghamshire, England, 1880s)

Just give me Arthur.

W. G. GRACE, asked to name his greatest contemporary batsman.

He never seemed to make runs – they came.

G. L. JESSOP.

Put me under the ground 22 yards from Arthur, so that I may send him a ball now and then.

ALFRED SHAW, asking to be buried near Arthur Shrewsbury, **1907**.

John Snow (Sussex, England)

His bowling performances and more especially his fielding have been so lacking in effort that the selection committee have no alternative.

Sussex selectors, dropping England's pace bowler John Snow, **1971**.

A really quick bowler when he wanted to be . . . Snow had the typical fast bowler's moodiness, and he was a bit of a loner.

BOB WILLIS, *The Cricket Revolution*, **1981**.

F. R. Spofforth (Australia)

A tall, rather slim figure, but lissom, wiry, and full of vitality; a very high action and an atmosphere of undisguised hostility, and a subtle and unresting brain behind it all. There was never a more thoughtful bowler than the Demon; it is said that he would often lie awake at night, turning over in his mind the best methods of attacking the great batsmen opposed to him . . . given the slightest help from the pitch he was beyond all doubt what the 'Demon' proclaimed him, the greatest bowler in the world.

H. S. ALTHAM, *A History of Cricket*, **1926**.

(He) possessed the temperament of a match-winner to a degree.

L. H. BACMEISTER, *The Cricketer*, **1928**.

His nickname, the Demon Bowler . . . appeared to be descriptive of his indefatigability at the critical moment of a match more than of his much rarer so-called 'lightning flashes'.

L. H. BACMEISTER.

David Steele (Northamptonshire, England)

A bank clerk going to war.

CLIVE TAYLOR, the *Sun*, as Steele defied West Indies pace bowlers, **1976**.

Mickey Stewart (Surrey)

He is representative of his time: an amateur type who became a professional.

PHIL PILLEY, *The Cricketer*.

Mickey's father . . . was, in fact, a London suburban bookmaker – and here, perhaps, is a hint of why Stewart has blended so easily into *professional* county cricket. He had become, so to speak, the amateur-type son of professional-type forbears.

PHIL PILLEY, *The Cricketer*.

Tom Sueter (Hambledon)

I have seldom seen a handsomer man than Tom Sueter, who measured about five feet ten. As if, too, Dame Nature wished to show at his birth a specimen of her prodigality, she gave him so amiable a disposition, that he was the pet of all the neighbourhood: so honourable a heart that his word was never questioned by the gentlemen who associated with him: and a voice, which for sweetness, power and purity of tone (a tenor), would, with proper cultivation, have made him a handsome fortune. With what rapture have I hung upon his notes when he has given us a hunting song in the club room after the day's practice was over.

JOHN NYREN, in *The Cricketers Of My Time*, **1833**.

Chris Tavaré (Kent, England)

When he strolls away towards square leg . . . it is like an act of thanksgiving that the previous ball has been survived and a moment of prayer for the fibre to get through the next.

BOB WILLIS, *The Captain's Diary*, **1983**.

Freddie Trueman (Yorkshire, England)

Without rival, the ripest, the richest, the rip-roaringest individual performer on cricket's stage.

A. A. THOMSON, *The Cricketer*, **1961**.

Fred not only bowled fast. He was a fast bowler to the very depths of his soul.

JOHN HAMPSHIRE, *Family Argument*, **1983**.

Fred Trueman the mature fast bowler was a sharply pointed and astutely directed weapon; Fred Trueman the man has often been tactless, haphazard, crude, a creature of impulse. In Fred Trueman the public image, so many accretions of rumour and fiction have been deposited round the human core that the resultant figure is recognisable only to those who do not know him.

JOHN ARLOTT in *Fred*, **1971**.

I had asked my publishers to call my biography 'T' Definitive Volume on t' Finest Bloody Fast Bowler that Ever Drew Breath'. But the silly buggers just intend to call it 'Fred'.

FRED TRUEMAN, **1971**.

His public were the customers whose quiet contemplation of their evening pint was suddenly converted, in an instant, into participation in the Greatest Show on (Cricket's) Earth. The one and only F. S. Trueman had arrived. Fred's jacket was suddenly thrust to the back of his shoulders, the chin jutted, the pipe projected even further as he hustled to the bar. Henry Irving never made greater impact with a stage entrance than Freddie Trueman in a pub.

JOHN HAMPSHIRE, *Family Argument*, **1983**.

Look, Freddie, you've got lots of pitches in Yorkshire, but if you keep on treading so heavily, Lancashire won't even have one.

Chairman of the Old Trafford ground committee to Freddie Trueman during England v India Test match, **1952**.

Tell me, Fred, have you ever bowled a ball which merely went straight?

RICHARD HUTTON, in exchange with Fred Trueman.

He is a genuine fast bowler, but his pace is not produced without considerable exertion. It is encouraging to think that Alf Gover . . . survived many dire prophecies of early thrombosis or rupture.

IAN PEEBLES, *Talking of Cricket*, **1953**.

Victor Trumper (Australia)

Victor Trumper had the greatest charm and two strokes for every ball.

C. B. FRY, *Life Worth Living*, **1939**.

Glenn Turner (Worcestershire, New Zealand)

I know the reason he likes the one-day game. He thinks it's great because nobody gets the ball above stump-high. We wouldn't tolerate that attitude in Australia.

KIM HUGHES. Turner's reply was that Hughes, and fellow Australian David Hookes, 'are simply block-bash merchants'.

Stuart Turner (Essex)

Best wishes from all those you have run out.

Inscription on 40th birthday cake to Stuart Turner from his Essex team-mates, **1983**.

Derek Underwood (Kent, England)

I must have kept wicket, day in day out, to Derek Underwood for seven years now and I doubt if he's bowled ten full-tosses or long-hops in the whole of that time.

ALAN KNOTT, **1972**.

The face of a choirboy, the demeanour of a civil servant and the ruthlessness of a rat catcher . . . Underwood is a mean pressure bowler who gives nothing away and expects nothing in return.

GEOFF BOYCOTT, *Opening Up*, **1980**.

In the old days I was considered miserly, and I'd settle for bowling maiden after maiden. These days there are times when it's vital to get a wicket – and my team-mates expect it of me as the senior bowler – so I experiment more.

DEREK UNDERWOOD, **1985**.

Hedley Verity (Yorkshire, England)

Hostility is not the same thing as say 'bodyline'. It marked Verity's bowling – he talked with his fingers – and he was a man who bowled as if in a mental abstraction, the batsman being the obstacle. He had that quality which never lets a batsman rest, never allows him an easy stroke, pinches him for foot space, makes him uneasy to step out in case he is stumped and haunts him with the feeling that he is going to be bowled round his legs by something he leaves alone.

WALTER HAMMOND.

Tom Walker (Hambledon, 1780s)

Those anointed clod-stumpers, the WALKERS, TOM and HARRY. Never sure came two such unadulterated rustics into a civilised community.

JOHN NYREN, *The Cricketers of My Time*. Tom Walker was Hambledon's wicket-keeper and one of cricket's first recorded stonewallers.

The driest and most rigid-limbed chap I ever knew, his skin was like the rind of an old oak, and as sapless. I have seen his knuckles handsomely knocked about from Harris's bowling; but never saw any blood on his hands – you might just as well attempt to phlebotomize a mummy.

JOHN NYREN, *The Cricketers of My Time*.

Cyril Washbrook (Lancashire, England)

I have never felt so glad in my life as when I saw who was coming in.

PETER MAY on Washbrook's entrance in his comeback match after a 5-year absence as England stood 17–3 v Australia at Headingley, **1956**.

Everton Weekes (West Indies)

Others punished my poorer balls, but Weekes, when in top form, could hit my good balls too.

RAY LINDWALL.

Gerry Weigall (Kent, 1890s)

Silhouetted against the dying sun can be seen illustrating every stroke in cricket with an umbrella. His umbrella was mainly used to give instructions in cricket, but for good measure he also used it for fencing, angling, showing us how Lindrum played his cushion canons and how King Edward VII put the gun to his shoulder for partridge.

ARTHUR MAILEY.

Bob Willis (Surrey, Warwickshire, England)

He was a star on the team coach: he seemed to know every dirty ditty that could ever have been sung in a Rugby club.

BOB TAYLOR, **1985**.

I don't go as far as that on my holidays.

Former Test bowler on the length of Bob Willis's run-up.

Bowler's name?

Cry from Edgbaston crowd, **1985**. Willis had taken only nine championship wickets, the previous year.

Charles Wright (Nottinghamshire, England, 1890s)

Was captain of Notts, and had also got a century in the University match. He was a most delightful person, but by no means the complete Encyclopaedia Britannica.

CYRIL FOLEY (Middlesex), *The Cricketer*, **1927**.

Well, I never! Here's Chals come all the way from Nottin'am to 'ave a friendly game with us, and you go and do a thing like that to 'im.

W. G. GRACE to his brother E.M., who had successfully appealed for hitting the ball twice after W.G. had asked Wright to knock the ball back to him. According to Foley, W.G. was part of the plot.

Frank Woolley (Kent, England)

Easy to watch, difficult to bowl to, and impossible to write about. When you bowled to him there weren't enough fielders; when you wrote about him there weren't enough words.

R. C. ROBERTSON-GLASGOW, *Cricket Prints*, **1943**.

The most graceful of the efficient, and the most efficient of the graceful.

I. A. R. PEEBLES, *Woolley – the Pride of Kent*, **1969**.

His cricket is compounded of soft airs and flavours. And the very brevity of summer is in it . . . The brevity in Woolley's batting is a thing of pulse and spirit, not to be checked by clocks, but only to be apprehended by imagination.

NEVILLE CARDUS, *Autobiography*, **1947**.

R. E. S. Wyatt (Warwickshire, Worcestershire, England)

I wasn't disputing your decision, Frank. I just couldn't believe that such an awful bowler could get me out twice.

FRANK WOOLLEY to umpire Frank Chester, when asked why he dallied at the crease after Wyatt dismissed him, Kent v Warwickshire at Dover, **1923**.

One of those valuable cricketers who are always doing something and doing it well.

SIR HOME GORDON, Bart.

Teams

Hambledon, 1770s/80s

No eleven in England could have had any chance with these men, and I think they might have beaten any twenty-two.

JOHN NYREN.

Troy has fallen and Thebes is a ruin. The pride of Athens is decayed, and Rome is crumbling to the dust. The philosophy of Bacon is wearing out, and the Victories of Marlborough have been overshadowed by greater laurels. All is vanity, but cricket; all is sinking in oblivion but you. Greatest of all elevens, fare ye well!

REV. JOHN MITFORD.

They were backbone players, ready to go till they dropped, and never sick or sorry in a match.

JOHN BOWYER (Surrey, The Players, England).

Cambridge University, 1830s

We never played in colours, and the men frequently failed to turn up. I don't think we had a captain in 1836!

R. J. P. BROUGHTON (Blue, 1836, 1838–9).

Oxford University, 1860s

There is frequently an uncertainty as to whose business it is to collect the XI; there are often two captains directing the field or changing the bowling.

Report of committee investigating Oxford cricket, **1862**. The club was run by three treasurers of equal responsibility.

Gloucestershire, 1920s

Only two problems with our team. Brewers' droop and financial cramp. Apart from that we ain't bloody good enough.

CHARLIE PARKER, Gloucestershire and England slow bowler (quoted by David Foot in *Cricket's Unholy Trinity*, **1985**).

Somerset, 1920s

For many of us, who had the luck and the honour to play for Somerset, memory lingers on of a hard but humorous adventure.

R. C. ROBERTSON-GLASGOW, *The Cricketer*.

Yorkshire, 1930s

Yorkshire cricket is soulless. Bowl six good-length balls and they're all pushed safely back. Decide to toss one higher and slower and, crash, it goes for four. After that, the same remorseless push, push, push, until you make another mistake.

'TUBBY' OWEN-SMITH of Middlesex **1937** (quoted by Bill Bowes in *Express Deliveries*, 1949).

Kent, 1940s/50s

I'm not so sure that success can only be measured in terms of matches won. For those who like the social side of cricket, whether as player or spectator, Kent cricket is the answer. Hospitality is readily extended in the various tents around the ground.

ARTHUR PHEBEY, Kent opening batsman of the period.

Australia, 1955

I don't think we'll ever see a better fielding side. Eight of your team ran like stags and threw like bombs.

PETER MAY, England captain, on Australians, 1955.

Surrey, 1950s

The spectator is fed up with seeing Laker and Lock, on helpful pitches, winning the County Championship for Surrey seven times in succession and making all international games in England a near farce.

W. E. BOWES, *The Cricketer*, 1959.

This team plays cricket in the way that it should be played. There is no hint of that depressing feature, sometimes seen on county grounds, of obviously Tired Tims for whom a six-day week is business rather than pleasure.

Times Editorial, August 1957.

West Indies, 1963

(They) have shown us once again that cricket can and should be played with either obvious delight or communicable disappointment – a human game – which is a truth that lay long and deeply hidden in certain countries that should know better.

R. C. ROBERTSON-GLASGOW.

We do not worry unduly about winning, losing or drawing. We wanted to impress the press and the public that our boys were pretty good cricketers and that they should come again much sooner than in 8 years' time – and I think we done that.

FRANK WORRELL at the end of the tour.

Sussex, 1963 (1st Gillette Cup Winners)

They are an enterprising batting side, of course, but as I see it their attack is perfect for 1963 conditions. They possess 5 accurate seam bowlers who give nothing away, with spinners Bell and Oakman making contributions on rare occasions.

COLIN COWDREY, *The Cricketer.*

Derbyshire, 1960s

Derbyshire batsmen always labour under certain difficulties both psychological and technical. They have no tradition to inherit, no heroes to emulate. They are regarded as subordinates, an inferior race with a secondary role; not much is expected of them and therefore not much is forthcoming. They know that 250 is enough in most games and therefore are incapable of aiming at higher totals. They bat just as well – or badly – on a bad wicket as a good one. Their aim is, by playing within their limitations, to scrape together enough runs to win matches.

GUY WILLATT, former Derbyshire player, **1970**.

Australia, 1970s/80s

The Australians have different standards and ways of expressing themselves – and swearing has been part of their approach on the field.

GLENN TURNER, **1983**.

It's going to be very hard to convince people back home that we really do have a lot of promising young players.

ALLAN BORDER after his 1985 side lost the Ashes.

Essex, 1970s/80s

That load of madmen will never win anything until they learn some self-discipline.

RAY ILLINGWORTH shortly before Essex won everything (quoted in Ray East, *A Funny Turn*, **1983**).

Pakistan, 1980s

They've always had a lot of talent, a lot of good players, but they're like eleven women. You know, they're all scratching each other's eyes out and wanting to do this and that. That has always been their downfall as a team.

IAN BOTHAM.

West Indies 1980s

In their disregard of anybody being hit and hurt some West Indians appeared callous and reminded me of bully boys.

JACK FINGLETON on the West Indies short-pitched bowling at the Oval, **1980**. Taken from *Batting From Memory*. **1981**

In the field the most boring team I had seen, with their super-abundance of fast bowlers who bowled so many bouncers (and therefore unplayable balls), their slow over rates with their incomprehensively long run-ups.

JACK FINGLETON, *Batting From Memory*.

England, 1980s

Getting like Glamorgan, isn't it? When the weak link in the side is the only Welshman.

Anon County Cricketer, on the number of South Africans playing for England.

If I was bowling against this England team, I'd get a lot more Test wickets than I did, they're bloody scared.

CHARLIE GRIFFITH, former West Indian pace bowler, during England's tour of Caribbean, **1981**.

The usual permutation of plebs: A few Gentlemen, some Professionals, a couple you'd rather not introduce to your mother – and at least one you'd cross Oxford Street to avoid.

FRANCES EDMONDS, *Daily Express*, **1985**.

2
Captains Courageous

A Captain's Lot

Why do so many players *want* to be captain?

DEREK UNDERWOOD (quoted by Mike Brearley in *The Art of Captaincy*, **1985**).

Cricket teams have often suffered from captains who have arrived, done queer things, departed and been forgotten.

R. C. ROBERTSON-GLASGOW, *Cricket Prints*, **1943**.

There is very little wrong that a captain cannot attend to.

STUART SURRIDGE, Surrey captain, in letter about the state of the game to the *Sunday Times*, **1957**.

It is a strange fact connected with cricket that a good captain is but seldom met with.

A. G. STEEL, *The Badminton Library – Cricket*, **1904**.

There never was a good skipper of a bad side. And I've got a great one. I could go out with any one of them tonight just as easily as I could with my wife.

JACK BOND on Lancashire, **1972**.

A public relations officer, agricultural consultant, psychiatrist, accountant, nursemaid and diplomat.

D. J. INSOLE's definition of a captain's duties.

It is easier for a football manager to 'play God', to read the riot act to the players, because he does not have to perform himself. Sales managers don't sell, foremen don't hump bricks. All cricket captains bat and field, and some bowl. We receive repeated intimations of our own fallibility.

MIKE BREARLEY, *The Art of Captaincy*, 1985.

I find I am playing every ball, bowling every ball and fielding every ball. The captaincy has cost me over six hundred runs a season. I am snapping at my wife and children and sleeping no more than four hours a night.

MICKEY STEWART, 1971, the year Surrey won the Championship.

As a county captain, one seems to spend an inordinate amount of time filling in forms of which no-one takes the slightest notice.

RAY ILLINGWORTH, *Yorkshire and Back*, 1980.

You're in charge from the moment you wake up until you buy a pint in the bar for the other players after the game. At times there are so many demands before play starts that I suddenly realise I've had no time for a knock-up myself.

M. C. J. NICHOLAS on his first season as captain of Hampshire, 1985.

The widely publicised mortality rate of managers of Football League clubs looks pretty insignificant when compared with the frequency with which county cricket captains go into liquidation.

D. J. INSOLE, *The Cricketer*, 1963.

The captaincy of a county side is no pushover, and the last man who thought it was has just recovered, happily, from an operation for a duodenal ulcer.

D. J. INSOLE, *The Cricketer*, 1963.

Mike Procter told me he had to leave the ground (Cheltenham) because of the amount of flak I was getting.

DAVID GRAVENEY, Gloucestershire, on his side's unhappy season, **1984**.

The player who stands at fine leg and occasionally refrains from admiring the female talent just long enough to castigate his captain for not changing the bowling is not recognisable as the same man when the onus of decisive action falls on him.

D. J. INSOLE.

Captaincy seems to involve half-hearing conversations which you'd rather not hear at all.

PETER ROEBUCK, Somerset batsman, in *It Never Rains*, **1984**.

I just hope people won't think I'm a swine and a rotter.

JOHN BARCLAY, Sussex skipper, declaring when Gehan Mendis was 96 not out and close to a county record, **1985**.

.Some skippers seem to be living in cloud-cuckoo land when they set their targets. I never cease to be amazed when a captain of a side that struggled to average two runs an over suddenly asks opponents to make in the region of eight runs an over to win.

RAY ILLINGWORTH, *Captaincy*, **1980**.

When I win the toss on a good pitch, I bat. When I win the toss on a doubtful pitch, I think about it a bit and then I bat. When I win the toss on a very bad pitch, I think about it a bit longer, and then I bat.

W. G. GRACE.

I suppose he got it for winning the toss.

BOB WILLIS, losing Warwickshire captain, after Lancashire's John Abrahams, who scored nought and did not bowl, won man-of-the-match award in Benson and Hedges Cup Final, **1984**.

I prefer to play under you for the season and pick up a few wrinkles.

LORD HAWKE, declining offer of captaincy from Tom Emmett after joining Yorkshire, **1882**.

My conscience is clear. Yorkshire had no chance of winning and my job was to prevent the other side from winning.

BRIAN CLOSE, after time wasting allegations which lost him the England captaincy, Warwickshire v Yorkshire at Edgbaston, **1967**.

I feel as if I had come third in an egg and spoon race at school and been awarded the prize because the first two had been disqualified.

COLIN COWDREY, assuming captaincy from Brian Close after time wasting controversy, **1967**.

England seem to have a fixation with so-called leadership qualities – and it usually means background.

GEOFFREY BOYCOTT, **1981**.

The rather involved wording of the statement issued to the press concerning the selection of England's cricket captain for the Test matches appealed to some people as a brilliant Bolshevist move on the part of the players selected. There was an idea, apparently, that the side would choose their own captain and play under him, or else loot the pavilion – any pavilion – seize the till, confiscate any portable property and burn the buildings.

The Cricketer, 'Notes and Comments', May **1921**.

No-one will follow a prig or a prude: but a captain cannot afford to be dissolute in his personal life.

MIKE BREARLEY, *The Art Of Captaincy*, **1985**.

If I become captain of Australia, I'll still swap the tops of salt and pepper shakers, put banana skins in players' boots and place pails above doors.

DAVID HOOKES, **1983**. He hasn't.

A 'keeper should be captain only on the rarest of occasions in first-class cricket. The mental strains of keeping wicket are just too much to be able to spend the time worrying about the nuts and bolts. The captain should be detached and analytical while it is the 'keeper's job to bawl out fielders and slap bowlers on the backside, telling them they're bowling well.

BOB TAYLOR, in *Standing Up, Standing Back*, **1985**.

What do they expect me to do? Walk round in a T-shirt with 'I'm in Charge' on it?

DAVID GOWER, responding to the selectors' vocal doubts about his restrained style of captaincy, **1986**.

Goodness knows what Simmons's thoughts were as he shared twelfth man duties with Clive Lloyd, unusual roles, incidentally, for a county's vice-captain and captain.

RICHARD STREETON, *The Times*, **1986**. Lloyd and Simmons had not been selected against Leicestershire in the first home match of the season.

They can all resign themselves to the fact that none of them will ever be quite as good as the talkative gentleman with the packet of ham sandwiches who sits square with the wicket on every county ground in the land.

D. J. INSOLE, on the fate awaiting the eight new county captains, **1963**.

Leaders of Men

G. O. (Gubby) Allen and D. R. Jardine (England)

Allowing for the relative skill of both sides, Allen got more out of his team than did Douglas Jardine. Allen was a keen student, so was Jardine, but where Jardine belonged to the atomic bomb era, Gubby fought his battles with pike and spears. When Gubby's battle ended, the noise and strife ended with it, but in the tough Scot's case, the 'death dust' lingered for a considerable time.

ARTHUR MAILEY.

Warwick Armstrong (Australia)

Often on a warm June afternoon on the mellow county grounds of England Warwick would doze at point and allow the game to drift like a ship left in the hands of its crew. There were very few batsmen in England in 1921 who could back-cut, and Warwick, after having a couple of glasses of ale at lunch, knew that there was a sanctuary in one part of the field where his siesta had little chance of being interrupted.

ARTHUR MAILEY.

To him reciprocity was a coward's weapon and he didn't have much time for arbitration, unless he himself could act as the arbitrator.

ARTHUR MAILEY.

Ian Botham (Somerset, England)

He captains the 'side like a great big baby.

HENRY BLOFELD, journalist, on Botham's leadership of England in West Indies, **1981**.

He always gets the benefit of my help. I haven't known him bothering asking much, have you?

GEOFFREY BOYCOTT, prior to West Indies tour, **1981**.

To appoint him to that position again would be to run the risk of reducing the greatest English cricketer since W. G. Grace from genius to mediocrity.

MIKE BREARLEY, on possibility of Botham returning to England captaincy, in *Phoenix From the Ashes*, **1982**.

Geoffrey Boycott (Yorkshire, England)

Brian Close's successor today as Yorkshire captain is Geoffrey Boycott, who is intelligent and highly technically informed. He has not Close's drive or flair, but he will make fewer mistakes and probably far fewer enemies.

JOHN ARLOTT in the *Guardian*.

He is so dedicated to the perfection and exploitation of his own batting technique that he is sometimes oblivious to the feelings and aspirations of his team-mates.

ARTHUR CONNELL, chairman of Yorkshire committee which replaced Boycott as captain, **1978**.

Sir Donald Bradman (Australia)

The Don, it appears, had two views of bouncers – one when they were bowled against him and the other when bowled by his side with no fear of retaliation.

JACK FINGLETON on Bradman's failure to dissuade Lindwall and Miller from excessive use of bouncers, **1946**; taken from *Batting From Memory*.

As a skipper he was merciless, determined from the outset in 1948 to get a record which meant as much as any to him – that of leading an unbeaten Australian team in England.

JACK FINGLETON, *Batting From Memory*. **1981**

Apart from (one instance) I never heard him praise a player unduly, or motivate his team with discussions of tactics. Perhaps his main resource as a leader was the example he set his men in concentration and the relentlessness of his attack.

JACK FINGLETON, *Batting From Memory*. **1981**

I didn't get on with him as a man. We had nothing in common. But as a batsman, captain and tactician, he had no equal.

KEITH MILLER.

Mike Brearley (Middlesex, England)

In Mike Brearley's unarrogant flat, where he lives alone – rumpled bedclothes in mid-afternoon and unwashed plates on the kitchen table – I made a beeline for the bookshelves. I spotted *Games People Play, The Divided Self, Human Aggression, The Art of Loving, Perspectives in Group Therapy, The Miracle Worker, The Poems of Auden*. I wonder what books Greig and Boycott have on their shelves?

DAVID BENEDICTUS.

He's got a degree in people, hasn't he?

RODNEY HOGG, Australian fast bowler.

On Friday I watched J. M. Brearley directing his fieldsmen very carefully. He then looked up at the sun and made a gesture which suggested that it should move a little squarer. Who is this man?

Letter to the *Guardian*, **1981**.

The statistics suggest that he is one of the great England captains. The luckiest would be nearer the truth.

RAY ILLINGWORTH on Brearley's first spell as England captain, **1980**.

That man must be a bigger ass than I thought he was.

CLIVE LLOYD replying to Brearley's criticisms of him as captain.

F. R. Brown (Northamptonshire, England)

Fine Lettuces! Hearts as big as Freddy Brown's!

Barrow boy outside Sydney, 5th Test Australia v England, **1951**.

F. R. Brown was of that type of Englishman not always finding favour in the dominions.

W. E. BOWES on Brown's management of the England team in Australia, **1958/9**; in *The Cricketer Spring Annual 1959*.

Ian Chappell (Australia)

Playing against a team with Ian Chappell as captain turns a cricket match into gang warfare.

MIKE BREARLEY, lecture at St John's College, Cambridge, **1980**.

There are some things about Ian Chappell I shouldn't have copied, like the way he always used to refuse to sign autographs in a bar. Here was me, 18, telling 50-year-olds to stuff off.

DAVID HOOKES, Australian batsman, **1983**.

Brian Close (Yorkshire, Somerset, England)

He played many useful innings, but probably his main accomplishment was that he kept the volatile and voluble Trueman happy.

BILL BOWES reviewing Close's first season as Yorkshire captain.

Eh, up, Raymond, t' rudder's gone again.

JIMMY BINKS, Yorkshire wicket-keeper, to Ray Illingworth on Close's tendency to let his mind wander.

There were times when Closey could make Walter Mitty appear a modest realist.

RAY EAST, from *A Funny Turn*, **1983**.

Herby Collins (Australia)

At heart Collins was a gambler. His hunting grounds were the racecourse, the dog-track, Monte Carlo, 'The Den of Thieves' (near the Strand 1921/6), a baccarat joint at King's Cross, a 'two-up' school in the Flanders trenches in World War I and anywhere a quiet game of poker was in operation. 'Mauldy' Collins gambled everywhere except on the cricket field, and on anything but cricket.

ARTHUR MAILEY.

As a batsman Collins was a miser; as a left-arm bowler, like Charles Macartney and Wilfred Rhodes, he was an even greater miser.

ARTHUR MAILEY.

M. C. Cowdrey (Kent, England)

He could never make up his mind whether to call heads or tails.

RAY ILLINGWORTH.

In view of the settled weather and the Manchester holidays next week, Mr Cowdrey will not necessarily enforce the follow-on if this situation arises.

G. HOWARD, Lancashire secretary, during Colin Cowdrey's first Test as England captain v India, **1959**.

Mike Denness (Kent, England)

Two Scots have captained England in Australia within the past 50 years – Douglas Jardine and Mike Denness. Jardine was a charming fellow who did not like Australians. Denness is a very charming fellow who is not yet in a position to know whether he likes Australians or not. But he'll know by the end of the tour.

SIR LEONARD HUTTON, BBC TV, **1974**.

Ted Dexter (Sussex, England)

There is no doubt that Dexter can handle a bat but who is going to handle Dexter?

England selector after appointment of Dexter as captain, **1962**.

J. W. H. T. Douglas (Essex, England)

He has many assets as a captain . . . but he cannot be called a great tactician as he occasionally takes time to see the obvious.

Portrait of Douglas in *The Cricketer* on his appointment to captain England v Australia, **1921**.

Well, if you're going to bowl with the new one, you can bloody well go on with the old one, too.

SYDNEY BARNES to Douglas, after he chose to take the new ball himself, MCC in Australia, **1911/12**.

Johnny used to bowl them in, then chuck the ball to me to bowl them out.

CECIL PARKIN, denied new ball by Douglas, on MCC tour of Australia, **1920/21**.

W. G. Grace (Gloucestershire, England)

There was an unwritten law prevailing in those days – a rule, I believe, confined to those under 'W.G.'s' leadership – which forbade any person or persons airing opinions on the game unless he or they had scored a century in first-class cricket. As in the majority of matches there was only one man on the side who had achieved the feat, we were not greatly troubled by listening to immature thoughts.

G. L. JESSOP on Gloucestershire under Grace.

The majority of our side were thoroughly in accord with the (umpire's) decision, but nothing would shake 'W.G.'s' contention, and for the rest of the day we all went about our tasks in hushed silence.

G. L. JESSOP on Grace's response to having a run-out appeal turned down after A. C. MacLaren trod on his wicket, Lancashire v Gloucestershire, Old Trafford, **1896**.

Tony Greig (Sussex, England)

He was the first England player I remember actively indulging in gamesmanship.

BOB TAYLOR, **1985**.

There's only one head bigger than Greig's – and that's Birkenhead.

FRED TRUEMAN.

If Greig fell off the Empire State Building, he'd land on a furniture van fitted with mattresses.

England colleague, **1976**.

What has to be remembered of course is that he is not an Englishman by birth or upbringing, but only by adoption. It is not the same thing as being English through and through.

JOHN WOODCOCK, *The Times* Cricket Correspondent, on Greig's defection to Packer when England captain.

He doesn't go with my idea of captaincy or decent behaviour.

GEORGE COX, Sussex player for 29 years, resigning from county committee when
Greig was reappointed captain in wake of Packer judgement, **1977**.

I have no respect for him as a cricketer or as a man.

IAN CHAPPELL, **1979**.

Ken Grieves (Lancashire)

Quite apart from various other perfectly sound reasons, his knowledge of the night-life of Manchester will make his reappearance
welcome among his opponents.

D. J. INSOLE, then a Test selector, on Grieves's return from league cricket to
captain Lancashire, **1963**.

Lionel Hallam, 3rd Baron Tennyson (Hampshire, England)

His earliest days were lived under two awe-inspiring shadows: of
Government House, Sydney . . . and of the ghost of the old Poet
Laureate, deep-voiced, shaggily bearded, stumping in cloak and
sombrero along the echoing corridors of Farringford. This sort of
upbringing might have been complex-fodder for the more regrettable type of modern novelist. But Lionel survived. If he had even
known what a complex was, he would have hit it over
Southampton pavilion for six.

A. A. THOMSON.

Yes, but he was a lovely man; just a big boy really.

PHILLIP MEAD on Tennyson's failings in captaincy.

Sir Len Hutton (Yorkshire, England)

The outstanding characteristic of his captaincy was shrewdness. He made no romantic gestures; he lit no fires of inspiration. He invited admiration rather than affection and would have exchanged both for effective obedience. A Test match rubber played under Hutton's captaincy became a business undertaking with its principal satisfactions represented by the dividends paid. Hutton did not expect his players to enjoy their Test matches until the scoreboard showed victory. He could not countenance a lighthearted approach to any cricket match when the result of that match had a meaning. He wanted his team-mates to be untiringly purposeful.

J. M. KILBURN. *Yorkshire Post* correspondent, on Hutton's retirement, in *The Cricketer*, **1956**.

Ray Illingworth (Yorkshire, Leicestershire, England)

The severest criticism of Ray Illingworth is that he did not sufficiently discourage the element of selfishness which is part of most professional cricketers.

MIKE BREARLEY, **1973**.

D. R. Jardine (Surrey, England)

A dour remorseless Scot, 130 years after his time. He should have gone to Australia in charge of a convict hulk.

JACK FINGLETON, Australian opening bat.

He is a queer fellow. When he sees a cricket ground with an Australian on it, he goes mad.

SIR PELHAM WARNER, letter to Governor of South Australia, **1934**, after the 'Bodyline' rumpus.

He can be a powerful friend but a relentless enemy. He gives no quarter and asks none. He is a fighter, every inch of him. He will see a job through, no matter what the consequences, and will never admit defeat.

BILL BOWES, *Express Deliveries*, **1949**.

Herbert Jenner (Cambridge)

Jenner, the Cambridge captain, made more runs than all his companions together, and also bowled from one end and kept wicket at the other.

Report of 1st Varsity match, **1827**, cited by FRANK MITCHELL, *The Cricketer*, **1927**.

What more could a captain do? Some captains only get a bowl when they are captain, but not many of them are very keen on acting as Aunt Sally.

FRANK MITCHELL on the above.

Graham Johnson (Kent)

Eminently suitable to be Kent's captain. He is a thoughtful and intelligent cricketer who must have made many followers of cricket less suspicious of the London School of Economics.

Daily Telegraph Leader, **1975**. Johnson was not appointed.

Roger Knight (Surrey)

Roger Knight is a smashing bloke but he's no captain. I asked him if I could do some bowling again and all I got was two balls when the other team needed two to win.

DAVID SMITH, leaving Surrey for Worcestershire, **1983**.

I told Knight it was like being back at school again with all that arm-waving.

DAVID SMITH, after a 'V-sign', when batting, to Knight led to his departure from Surrey, **1983**.

Clive Lloyd (Lancashire, West Indies)

This was not great captaincy, it was barbarism.

SUNIL GAVASKAR, on Lloyd's handling of West Indian pace attack, **1976**.

Without being unkind, a donkey could lead West Indies at the moment. But put Clive Lloyd in charge of Australia and even he'd struggle.

KEITH FLETCHER, reacting to Hughes's resignation of Australian captaincy, **1984**.

A. C. MacLaren (Lancashire, England)

A pessimistic commander. I have heard old timers say he was liable to enter the dressing-room clutching his head and saying 'Look what they've given me this time,' or 'Gracious me! Don't tell me you're playing!' which cannot have been very good for morale.

IAN PEEBLES.

England may have.had worse captains, but I would be hard put to it to name two or three.

ALAN GIBSON, *The Times* on the centenary of MacLaren's birth, **1971**.

P. B. H. May (Surrey, England)

Everyone knows, after Australia, that May is no squealer, no matter how provoked.

ROBIN MARLAR on the controversial **1959/60** 'chucking' tour.

Keith Miller (Australia)

One of you bugger off, and the rest scatter.

KEITH MILLER, captaining New South Wales, when told he had 12 players on the field.

M. J. K. Smith (Warwickshire, England)

His approach to a problem was to sit in a chair with the *Daily Telegraph* crossword, doze off, wake up, finish the crossword and then fire some broadsides.

COLIN COWDREY, in *MCC*, **1976**.

Sir Gary Sobers (Nottinghamshire, West Indies)

I've only one objection to Gary Sobers as skipper. He doesn't work me hard enough by half. When he tells me I must be tired after bowling for an hour or so and then takes me off it makes me laugh. I haven't even worked up a sweat by then.

DAVE HALFYARD, returning to county cricket for Notts at the age of 37 after recovering from a road accident, **1968**.

Bob Willis (Surrey, Warwickshire, England)

I am a born pessimist.

BOB WILLIS, *The Captain's Diary*, **1983**.

3

The Game that Was

Cricket Through the Ages

As a scholler in the free school of Guildeford he and several of his fellowes did run and play there at cricket and other plaies.

Testimony of JOHN DERRICK, gent, during reign of Henry VIII, **1549**.

I present Ralph West, Edmund Hartley, Richard Slaughter, William Martin, Richard Martin Junior, together with others whose names I have no notice of, for playing at Cricket in the Churchyard on Sunday, the fifthe of Maye, after sufficient warning had been given to the contrarie, for three special reasons: first, for it is contrarie to the 7th Article; second, that they are used to break the Church windows with their balls; and thirdly, for that little children had like to have their braynes beaten out with the cricket batt.

Indictment of the above at Chichester Assizes by a Churchwarden from Boxgrove Deanery, **1622**.

Two Londoners striving for expedition to gain the ball, met each other with such fierceness, that, hitting their heads together, they both fell backwards without stirring hand or foot, and lay deprived of sense for a considerable time, and 'tis not yet known whether they will recover.

Report on London v Kent at Islington, **1720**, in *The Postman*. London won.

Ye pitching of ye first Wicket is to be determined by ye cast of a piece of Money.

Law 1, first code of rules, **1744**.

If ye Wicket is Bowled down, its Out.

First code of rules, **1744**; Laws for Ye Strikers.

When ye Ball has been in hand by one of ye Keepers or Stopers, and ye Player has been at home, He may go where he pleases till ye next ball is bowled.

First code of rules, **1744**.

Lords and gentleman, clergymen and lawyers . . . associate themselves with butchers and cobblers in such diversions.

The British Champion, **1743**, criticizing cricket matches.

(These matches) draw numbers of people from their employment to the ruin of their families. It brings together crowds of apprentices and servants whose time is not their own. It propagates a spirit of idleness at a juncture when, with the utmost industry, our debts, taxes, and decay of trade will scarce allow us to get bread.

The British Champion, **1743**.

It (cricket) is a most notorious and shameless breach of the laws, as it gives the most open encouragement to gambling.

The British Champion, **1743**.

Cricket is certainly very innocent and wholesome exercise, yet it may be abused, if either great or little people make it their business. It is grossly abused when it is made the subject of publick advertisements, to draw together great crowds of people, who ought, all of them, to be somewhere else. Noblemen, gentlemen and clergymen have certainly a right to divert themselves in what manner they think fit; nor do I dispute their privilege of making butchers, cobblers or tinkers their companions, provided they are qualified to keep their company. But I very much doubt whether they have any right to invite thousands of people to be spectators of their agility at the expense of their duty and honesty. The time of people of fashion may be indeed of very little value, but in a trading country the time of the meanest man ought to be of some worth to himself and to the community.

The Gentleman's Magazine, **1744**.

Numbers of my friends have intimated that the taking of Six-pence admittance has been very prejudicial to me; these (notices) are to inform them that for the future they shall be admitted for Two-pence, and the favour of their Company greatly acknowledged by Their very humble servant, George Smith.

Notice posted by the owner of the HAC ground, George Smith, after an increase in admission from 2d to 6d had caused a fall in gates from around 7,000 to 200, **1744**.

The Town may be certain that the taking of Six-pence admittance is. out of no avaricious Temper, Two-pence being greatly insufficient to the Charge that attends the matches, which Mr Smith is ready to make appear to any Gentleman.

Smith's notice explaining the rise in admission prices again, **1747**.

Cricket is, to be sure, a manly game and not bad in itself, but it is the ill-use made of it, by betting above £10 upon it, that is bad and against the laws.

Judge's comment during a lawsuit over a betting debt, **1748**.

I could tell you of Lord Montfort's making cricket matches and fetching up parsons by express from different parts of England to play on Richmond Green.

HORACE WALPOLE, **1749**.

A young fellow, a butcher, being entrusted with about £40 by his mistress to buy cattle in Smithfield Market, instead went into the Artillery Ground and sported away the whole sum in betting on the cricket players.

St James's Chronicle, **1765**.

A wet day, only three members present, nine bottles of wine.

Extract from early minutes of Hambledon club.

Half the county would be present, and all their hearts with us. Little Hambledon pitted against All England was a proud thought for the Hampshire men. Defeat was glory in such a struggle – Victory, indeed, made us only a 'little lower than angels'.

JOHN NYREN on cricket at Hambledon, **1780s**.

The roar that followed Mann's celebrated hit never is to be forgotten; it was like the running of a cataract; it came pouring from a thousand lungs.

REV. JOHN MITFORD on a shot for 10 by Noah Mann.

Many (attend) out of compliment to Sir Horace . . . and, as he gives a very magnificent ball and supper on Friday, it would not be so polite to attend that without paying a compliment to his favourite amusement.

Letter from Lady Hales to Mrs Phillips (Susan Burney) explaining why Hampshire society turned up en masse for Sir Horace Mann' match v Duke of Dorset, **1782**.

We . . . do agree to meet upon Heworth Moor every Tuesday and Friday morning at 4 o'clock until the Fifth day of September next, for the purpose of playing cricket.

York CC's inaugural rules, **1784**.

We are happy to hear that the report of Mr Louch's being killed
at Bourne Paddock by a ball from the point of the bat, struck
with such force that it lodged in his body, is devoid of foundation.
Yet the melancholy tale occasioned some debates in the club
whether the striker was fairly out.

Report of the injury to George Louch (Kent) in match v Hampshire, **1789**. It
was widely believed including by his team mates that Louch had been killed.

Deth minds a krikketer no more
Than he does cracking nuts
Louch could not stop the ball before
he cocht hur in his Guts.

Epitaph on Louch's 'demise' by a Kent colleague.

Descending to the office of a coachman and driving his own
carriage is not altogether compatible with a high rank and station,
the more so when it is done in a public manner. The making of
his own lamplighter a partner at a game of cricket is equally
censurable.

The Times, **1788**, on the behaviour of a Brighton gentleman.

Although we have all on occasions enjoined proper muscular
exercise, yet we strongly reprobate that of cricket, which is in all
respects too violent, and, from the positions into which players
must necessarily throw themselves, cannot fail to be productive
of frequent injury to the body. Indeed, we have witnessed several
melancholy accidents which lately happened in our neighbourhood; from the awkward posture occasioned by employing both
arms at the same time in striking a distant object.

Dr Willich's Domestic Encyclopaedia, **1802**.

Cricket is unalloyed by love of lucre and mean jealousies . . . the
approbation and applause of the spectators being the sole reward.

LORD FREDERICK BEAUCLERK, speech to Thatched House Tavern, **1838**.

Few were the matches I did not win, for I always had one principle to guide me, and that was to get the two best bowlers and the best wicket-keeper, and let the batting take its chance, comparatively.

HENRY KINGSCOTE (MCC President 1927) on picking England XIs to play county sides at Lord's.

The Kent people thought we had sold the match which, of course, was nonsense; but Alfred Mynn was hissed in Maidstone Market.

SIR EMILIUS BAYLEY on Kent's defeat by All England by 9 wickets after scoring 278 in their first innings at Canterbury, **1840**.

Cricket grounds be laid out at each end of the barrack stations throughout the United Kingdom for the use of officers and privates.

Order by THE DUKE OF WELLINGTON, Commander in Chief, **1841**.

We got up a tolerably good match behind the Hotel Royal, on the beach at Dieppe, for the amusement of the Duchess de Berri, in the year 1829. We mustered, with some difficulty, two elevens; the bowlers pitched their balls with scientific precision; the batters defended their wickets with great skill; short and long stops were on the alert; in fact, all the performers acquitted themselves most admirably. As soon as the first innings were over, one of the party who had been most active in the display of his athletic powers, approached the Duchess' carriage in the expectation of being complimented on his exertions; instead of which, one of the suite asked the gentleman, to his utter dismay and confusion, when this game of *creekay* was going to begin!

The Times, **1841**.

I went out into the country, and had the pleasure of seeing a match of cricket, in which a noble earl, the Lord Lieutenant of his county, was playing with the tradesmen, the labourers and all around him, and I believe that he lost no respect from that course – they loved him better, but they did not respect him less. I believe that if they themselves associated more with the lower classes of society, the kingdom of England would be in a far safer, and society in a far sounder, condition.

BARON ALDERSON, addressing grand jury of Suffolk, **1844**.

I never played at Lord's in a match in which we did not have to run all our hits out. Considerable crowds used to come to see the matches, and when the ball went among the spectators, the fielders had to go after it and find it. Even in my last match for the Gentlemen at Lord's in 1868, there was no boundary.

R. A. H. MITCHELL, from W. A. Bettesworth's *Chats on The Cricket Field*, **1892**.

Their (boundaries) gradual introduction, dating from the (18)60s, had an adverse effect on deep fielding, and especially on throwing, to which the simultaneous urbanisation of the country also contributed.

H. S. ALTHAM, *A History of English Cricket*, **1926**.

It was a serious thing not to stop a hard hit when the ball had to be followed until it was overtaken, and many balls used to be stopped which are now allowed to pass by as 'it is only 4'.

R. A. H. MITCHELL, from W. A. Bettesworth's *Chats on The Cricket Field*, **1892**.

Even when a man is in most perfect condition he is a little pumped when he has run a fiver or a sixer, and numberless wickets have been lost because a man was too pumped to be able to play the next ball with confidence after a big hit.

V. E. WALKER, from W. A. Bettesworth's *Chats on The Cricket Field*, **1892**.

CRICKET RULES Drawn up by the Nottinghamshire County Cricket Club 1863/4.

Rule 1: That in playing Lancashire, the Lancashire men shall not be allowed to use bats but only broom handles.
Rule 2: That Lancashire should not be allowed any bowlers, and if so no stumps be used; and the Notts captain to select the bowler.
Rule 3: That both umpires be strictly Notts men.
Rule 4: That in case there is any fear that Notts should lose, even under these rules, the Notts men do leave the field and refuse to finish the game.

Lancashire Christmas card to Nottinghamshire, **1863**.

LANCASHIRE COUNTY CRICKET
The only rules necessary for players in the County Eleven are that
they should neither have been born in, nor reside in, Lancashire.
Sutton-in-Ashfield men will have the preference.

Nottinghamshire New Year retort, **1864**.

The telephone is a splendid invention, speaking generally, but I
cannot help wishing it had never been utilised on the cricket field.
The falling off of gates is, I believe, in a measure owing to this.

RICHARD DAFT, **1893**.

Men stand in the field today like so many 'little mounds of earth'
. . . the energy, the life, the ever-watchfulness of 10 years ago are
gone, and in their place are lethargy, laziness and a wonderful
yearning for rest.

Wisden, **1901**.

Audun struck the ball over Grettir's head, so that he could not
reach it. Grettir . . . fetched the ball, brought it back, and, going
up to Audun, drove it straight into his forehead, so that the skin
was broken. Audun then struck at Grettir with the bat he was
holding.

Saga of Grettir The Strong (1010), cited in letter to *The Cricketer*, **1927**.

The Midfjord cricket week of 1010 is, indeed, a strange thought.
Iceland had been colonised from Norway rather more than 100
years before, and at about the same period when other Norsemen
and Danes were making their own all that part of England north
of a line from Chester to London. Can it be to them that we owe
the game, as we owe so much else? Can Yorkshire trace her
prowess to the fact that she is the most purely Norse of all English
counties?

Letter to *The Cricketer*, **1927**.

The crux of his thesis (Cricket in the Bible) turns on the request of St Peter: 'Send me not into the deep, as I have toiled all day and caught nothing'.

R. C. ROBERTSON-GLASGOW 'The Origins of Cricket: A Monograph', *The Cricketer*, **1927**.

This modern scoffing at tradition is a product of super-democracy. Tradition is a hell of a good thing. It's what takes a regiment through hell.

PELHAM WARNER, **1933**.

W. G. Grace was a Victorian but the game he transformed into a national institution was not Victorian either in origin or essence. It was a creation of pre-Victorian England . . . the England of the early Dickens and of William Hazlitt. It was an England still unconquered by the Industrial Revolution. It travelled by saddle and carriage. Whenever it could, it ate and drank prodigiously. It was not finicky in morals. It enjoyed life . . . There were rulers and rules, the educated and the uneducated.

C. L. R. JAMES, Marxist historian, in *Beyond a Boundary*, **1963**.

4

The Beautiful Game

Styles, Standards and Lifestyles

Ye gods, is the game to be ruled by young men, some of whom are prepared to take the unwritten law into their own hands?

LORD HAWKE, following first artificial declaration in first-class cricket, Gloucestershire v Yorkshire, **1931**.

You do well to love it, for it is more free from anything sordid, anything dishonourable than any game in the World. To play it keenly, honourably, generously, self-sacrificingly is a moral lesson in itself, and the class-room is full of God's air and sunshine. Foster it, my brothers, so that it may attract all who can find the time to play it; protect it from anything that would sully it, so that it may grow in favour with all men.

LORD HARRIS's speech to half-holiday cricketers (quoted in letter to *The Times* on his 80th birthday, **1931**).

What can you have better than a nice green field, with the wickets set up, and to go out and do the best for your side.

GEORGE HIRST in his retirement speech at Scarborough, **1921**.

Foreigners suspect that cricket is a form of English lunacy. They will never understand there is a method in this English madness. It is what keeps them sane.

ANDRE DRUCKER.

In Affectionate Remembrance
of
ENGLISH CRICKET
which died at the Oval
on
29th August, 1882.

Deeply lamented by a large circle of
Sorrowing Friends and Acquaintances
R.I.P.
N.B.– The body will be cremated, and the
Ashes taken to Australia.

Sporting Times obituary which began the story of 'The Ashes'.

To some people cricket is a circus show upon which they may or may not find it worthwhile to spend sixpence; to others it is a pleasant means of livelihood; to others a physical fine art full of plot, interest and enlivened by difficulties; to others in some sort it is a cult and a philosophy.

C. B. FRY, Foreword to D. L. A. Jephson's *A Few Overs*, **1913**.

Cricket is indescribable. How do you describe an orgasm?

GREG MATTHEWS (Australia).

An expedition against bargemen or a match at cricket may be very pretty things to recollect, but, thank my stars, I can remember things very near as pretty.

HORACE WALPOLE looking back on his schooldays at Eton.

'If you have a right ambition, you will desire to excel all boys at cricket as well as in learning.'

LORD CHESTERFIELD in a letter to his son then at Eton, **1740s**.

Personally, I have always looked upon cricket as organised loafing.

WILLIAM TEMPLE, later Archbishop of Canterbury and then headmaster of Repton School, **1925**.

Even those who are very good and noble, say next door to angels, turn so rash and inconsiderate at certain moments that their brains lose the balance and begin to take fallacious fancies . . . Now, will you guess the cause of all this confusion and complexity? Assuredly it is nothing but the utter ignorance of the rules and methods, regards and respects of the game they have engaged in.

MOHUMMUD ABDULLAH KHAN, *Introduction to Cricket Guide*, Lucknow, **1891**.

The very word 'cricket' has become a synonym for all that is true and honest. To say 'that is not cricket' implies something underhand, something not in keeping with the best ideals.

SIR PELHAM WARNER.

To play cricket is synonymous with running straight.

EARL OF DERBY at Lancashire's Championship Dinner, **1926**.

In a desperate state of the game, every manoevre must be tried.

JOHN NYREN.

Any device or excuse is legitimate that may delay the game and the strikers thus become cold and inactive.

JOHN NYREN advocating gamesmanship to disturb strikers' concentration.

One could not be too particular when playing twenty-two.

TOM LOCKYER, All England XI wicket-keeper replying to criticism for tricking an opponent to leave his ground.

Use every weapon within the rules, and stretch the rules to breaking point, say I.

FRED TRUEMAN, **1961**.

We are perfectly entitled to prepare a surface which suits us and makes it more difficult for them. When England go to the West Indies next winter we have to take the type of pitches they give us – and you can be quite sure they will not be turners.

GEOFFREY BOYCOTT, **1981**.

The English have the irritating habit of appealing in chorus at every possible opportunity, presumably with the motive of discommoding the batsman. The sooner this undesirable habit is corrected the better.

Adelaide Advertiser, on Shrewsbury's England team in Australia, **1884**.

The team were also urged to improve its appealing, an area in which the Australians are undoubtedly superior. When appealing the Australians make a statement: we ask a question.

VIC MARKS, Somerset and England all-rounder, describing team meeting during tour of Australia, **1982/3**.

Behave like 'gentlemen' after the game is over, avoid clapping and laughing in faces of the persons you have defeated.

MOHUMMUD ABDULLAH KHAN, *Introduction to Cricket Guide*, Lucknow, **1891**.

Ah, cricket, the sight of bowler and players genuinely applauding a century against them. If a Rangers soccer side stood to applaud a Celtic goal I'd know the age of miracles had come. Cricket's greatness lies in the ability of players to honour a foe. It's the way life should be lived.

PROF. WILLIAM BARCLAY.

I was surprised to find, after sampling the fare at Twickenham, that the Oxford and Cambridge sides do speak to each other before and during the game at Lord's.

TONY LEWIS, Cambridge captain, **1962**.

I may not make myself popular saying it, but the decline of cricket as a character builder has had a lot to do with our present situation. As soon as soccer became the so-called national sport, the whole idea of a game that was played for its own sake among people who understood each other went by the board.

FREDERICK RAPHAEL, **1973**.

Right: 'The coming of Ranji rather upset the "off theory" business.' G.L.Jessop

Below: 'The elegant and scientific game of cricket will degenerate into a mere exhibition of rough, coarse, horse-play.' John Nyren on the consequences of allowing round-arm bowling, as demonstrated here by Roger Iddison

Above: 'He made utility the criterion of style.' Ranji on W.G. Grace

Left: 'Essentially the "Big Man" at Lord's, and what MCC would do without him, I do not know.' Pelham Warner on Lord Harris

Right: 'My word, Herbert, if it hadn't been for my lumbago, we'd have brayed 'em.' Percy Holmes to Herbert Sutcliffe after record opening partnership of 555 v. Essex, 1932

Facing page: 'No bugger ever got all ten when I was at the other end.' Sydney Barnes on Jim Laker's feat of taking 19 wickets in the Fourth Test v. Australia, Old Trafford, 1956

Below: 'There are two teams out there; one is trying to play cricket and the other is not.' Bill Woodfull, Australian captain, during the bodyline series

Top: 'I was shocked at the male chauvinism which has survived. I had to sit in the Tavern stand. The MCC should change their name to MCP.' Diana Edulji, Indian women's captain, on being banned from the Lord's pavilion, England v. India 1986

Above: 'We've always set the trend. Remember, women cricketers were the first to bowl overarm.' Rachel Heyhoe-Flint

I got a terrible surprise when he kicked me. I lifted my bat to ward him off and to tell him that if he hit me, I would hit him . . . he kept saying dirty words to me.

JAVED MIANDAD, Pakistan batsman, kicked by Australian pace bowler Dennis Lillee, Perth, **1981**.

Javed Miandad is no angel. He's an irritating little character who keeps baiting people.

TONY GREIG on the same incident.

If we found that Dennis was the instigator, we would have rubbed him out.

GREG CHAPPELL, Australian captain, explaining £100 fine imposed by players' disciplinary committee after Lillee kicked Javed Miandad during Test match against Pakistan, **1981**.

Just remember one thing son, you've already been killed once on a cricket field.

IAN BOTHAM's warning to Ewen Chatfield after the New Zealand seamer had run out Derek Randall while backing up. Christchurch Test, **1977/8** tour.

When Randall was run out backing up I thought that if it had been my school the bowler would have been beaten for it by the housemaster – and quite right too.

PHIL EDMONDS on New Zealand v England, **1977/8**.

You know a few Afrikaans swear words. Have·a go at him.

IAN BOTHAM to Allan Lamb during Wessels' 162 Australia v England, Brisbane, **1982/3**.

Whichever side it may be – and I fancy Eton were the principal offenders – the growing tendency towards ebullitions of affectionate exuberance in the field must be severely checked. They are not pretty at Wembley, but at Lord's quite intolerable.

'GHMC' on Eton v Harrow, *The Cricketer*, **1955**.

When I see a young man who has an expensive and pretty hair-do, I have doubts as to his ability to reach Test standard.

TED DEXTER, in *A Walk To The Wicket*, **1985**.

Innovations invariably are suspect, and in no quarter more so than the cricket world.

G. L. JESSOP.

Cricket, to maintain its hold on the national character, must be eager, quick and full of action. Today it is the reverse.

A. G. STEEL, *Wisden*, **1900**.

These bowlers might run people out, or stump them out, or catch them out, but they can't bowl to bowl anyone out; that bowling isn't mediogrity (sic)!

WILLIAM LILLYWHITE on the bowlers of **1840s/50s**.

In those days bowlers bowled a length for batsmen to make strokes, and such rubbish as leg theories on perfect wickets was not indulged in then.

A. C. MACLAREN on Tom Richardson's unchanged 3¼-hour spell of 6–76 in 42.3 overs as Australia scored 125–7 v England at Old Trafford, **1896**.

There were batting giants in the land then, and not two-eyed stance 'tragedies' patting singles and piling up leg-byes.

R. O. EDWARDS in *The Cricketer*, **1921**, harking back to the Golden Age of Grace.

Incidentally there were also wicket-keepers, not glorified armour-plated long stops . . .

R. O. EDWARDS, as above.

Over after over was bowled outside the off-stump in the hope that the batsman would make a mistake. Some did; others, profiting by experience, refused to be led into temptation, and consequently some very boresome periods eventuated.

G. L. JESSOP on the same period.

Where are the Batsmen?

The Cricketer, editorial headline, **1963**, in the days of May, Cowdrey, Dexter, M. J. K. Smith, Graveney and Barrington.

They now look for clowns not cricketers.

SYDNEY BARNES on northern leagues' increasing stress on 'showman' professionals, **1929**.

You don't know anything about it, it's a different game today.

YORKSHIRE PLAYER, to retired seam bowler Tony Nicholson, **1981**.

When the old hands complain that the batsmen of their day would have murdered Ramadhin and put Laker on the defensive they have right on their side. Their only mistake was to believe that that style of play can be invoked at will. It was more than a method, it was a philosophy of life.

C. L. R. JAMES, *Beyond A Boundary*, **1963**.

The gap in application between the earlier greats and their lesser contemporaries was far, far greater than the one between today's Test and county cricketers. It is not that modern top-line cricketers are inferior to their predecessors, it is that the post-war average county cricketer has raised his game.

PETER WALKER, *The Cricketer*, **1963**.

For thorough enjoyment, Test matches were too deadly serious. One always had the feeling of sitting on a barrel of gunpowder in contiguity to a lighted match and at the mercy of an untoward puff of wind.

G. L. JESSOP.

One may scoff at the idea of the Test match temperament, but it is a very real thing. The greatness of the occasion before now has accounted, I'll be bound, for almost as many failures as the greatness of the attack.

G. L. JESSOP.

Most people looking at the game from the outside cannot hope to appreciate the strain involved. Each Test match is a week full of pressure. I notice it more when new players join the England side. Take Les Taylor – he is a very experienced cricketer, yet the transition to Test level took him by surprise. He felt a difference in the atmosphere and tension, and like all newcomers found himself drained of energy more quickly than usual.

DAVID GOWER, **1985**.

In the Tests I sometimes break out into a sweat just putting on me boots. You'd be really surprised at how many players are nervous out there.

MIKE HENDRICK.

I don't actually enjoy Test cricket that much.

CHRIS TAVARÉ after making 35 in 5½ hours at Madras, England tour of India, **1981/2**.

A Test match contest is no kid-glove affair, and as a bat is a weapon of defence as well as attack, a first-class batsman, especially on modern-day wickets, should be able to deal safely with fast bowling, no matter of how short a length.

G. L. JESSOP, *The Cricketer*, **1921**.

This is a Test match. It's not Old Reptonians versus Lymeswold, one off the mark and jolly good show.

DAVID GOWER, England's captain, refusing to condemn Malcolm Marshall's use of bouncers during fifth Test v West Indies, **1984**.

Before they went in C. T. Studd was walking round the pavilion with a blanket over him; A. G. Steel's teeth were all in a chatter; and Billy Barnes's teeth would have been had he not left them at home.

TED PEATE on the scene in the England dressing-room during the 4th innings of the Test, **1882**. Asked to score 85, England lost by 2 runs!

I couldn't trust Mr Studd.

TED PEATE, Yorkshire professional and No. 11, last out, having a slog, in the same match. Studd was to some one of the best amateur batsmen of the time.

> Well done, Cornstalks, whipt us
> Fair and square.
> Was it luck that tripped us?
> Was it scare?
> Kangaroo land's 'Demon', or our own
> Want of devil, coolness, nerve, backbone?

Punch on England's defeat at The Oval, **1882**.

I've never been a good professional cricketer . . . I'm bloody marvellous for three days on the trot, very good for another day, but, in terms of concentration, not so hot for the next two or three.

TONY LEWIS, **1972**.

There are 250 players in county cricket. All are on first name terms, all know the other 249's strengths and faults in the techniques of the game, and play on these failings, thus resulting in lower totals more slowly accumulated.

PETER WALKER (Glamorgan, England), **1961**.

There is an enormous amount of mediocrity in English cricket. A lot of very average players are making their living out of the game when really they shouldn't be in it.

RICHARD HADLEE, in *At The Double*, **1985**.

All cricketers have large egos. That is why there are so many below average players still in the game. Each player secretly believes that he is a better cricketer than perhaps his results show.

PETER WALKER.

Although one's own side may be winning, there is no substitute for doing well personally. The game breeds moody players. Some just hide it better than others.

PETER WALKER.

The pest of the cricket field is the man who bores you about his average – his wickets – his catches; and looks blue even at the success of his own party. If unsuccessful in batting or fielding, he 'shuts up' – 'the wretch concentrated all in self'.

REV. JAMES PYCROFT, *The Cricket Field*, **1851**.

Players cannot be as selfish as they used to. Before, people used to play in order to be satisfied with their own performance. These days, you pick a team of workers and you would beat the teams of the past that had five stars who did it all.

JACK BOND, Lancashire team manager, **1985**.

England won't improve in world terms until the younger players rediscover some professional pride.

BOB TAYLOR, in *Standing Up, Standing Back*, **1985**.

The modern cricketer is not an ogre, nor is he deliberately obstructive. Although in most cases it would be unfair to dismiss him as a spoiled brat, he is too often lazy, ill-disciplined and reluctant to put in the effort and dedication commensurate with the wages he is earning. He has a very low boredom threshold with a constant need to be told what to do with his time.

BOB WILLIS, in *Lasting The Pace*, **1985**.

Certainly you are not going to face a cannon ball or hear the ugly sentence of your death, but on the other hand you are going to examine your own ability and capacity as a striker.

MOHUMMUD ABDULLAH KHAN's advice to batsmen to 'school himself into patience' before going to the wicket, *Introduction to Cricket Guide*, **1891**.

Batting is a major trial before an eleven-man jury.

RICHIE BENAUD.

I should like to say that good batsmen are born, not made; but my long experience comes up before me, and tells me that it is not so.

W. G. GRACE, *Cricket*, **1891**.

Find out where the ball is. Go there. Hit it.

RANJI's three precepts of batsmanship.

Tha knows one thing I learned about cricket: tha can't put in what God left out. Tha' sees two kinds of cricketers, them that uses a bat as if they are shovelling muck and them that plays proper and like as not God showed both of 'em how to play.

WILFRED RHODES, from Michael Parkinson's *Cricket Mad*, **1969**.

Any fool can play forward.

A. C. MACLAREN, *The Cricketer*, **1921**.

Nerves play as important a part in batsmanship as skill.

G. L. JESSOP.

Before I bat, I listen to the music of Midnight Oils, an Australian group a cross between Deep Purple and Bruce Springsteen.

GREG MATTHEWS, the disco kid, Australian all-rounder.

Between overs and at intervals or a break in play I kept my concentration by thinking about things like mowing the lawn.

TIM ROBINSON on his 175 v Australia, Headingley, **1985**.

Don't give advice to a batsman going in; if he's inexperienced, it will only make him nervous; if he is an old hand, it is generally unnecessary. Give him credit and opportunity to use his own judgement; if he doesn't do so at first, he soon will.

GILBERT JESSOP, in Foreword to James Thorpe's *Cricket Bag*, 1929.

To stand ideally is either to inflict upon yourself a form of astigmatism or of painful neck wrenching.

A. E. KNIGHT, *The Complete Cricketer*, **1906**.

If he (the batsman) uses the 'one-eyed' stance, it is a case for variation of pace. The reason . . . is that the bridge of his nose now intercepts the sight of his right eye and he is really looking at the ball only with one eye, which means the ball during its flight seems nearer to him than it is; the ball only gets into the proper focus at a point well on its journey.

F. R. SPOFFORTH in G. W. Beldham and C. B. Fry's *Great Bowlers*, **1906**.

Of course it would be absurd to suggest that those who have grown accustomed to bat left-handed could change in riper years. But there is much to be said for the suggestion of a rule that, say, after the year 1925 no one should come into cricket as a left-handed batsman. The result would be that all boys from now onwards be taught to bat right-handed; the left-handed batsmen now playing would automatically disappear in the process of time, and left-handed batting would cease to exist.

Article in *The Times*, **1913**.

I could never read the scores on the board . . . the specialist said to me: 'Who leads you out to bat?'

NEIL HARVEY, Australian batsman, admitting defective eyesight.

You don't need footwork in batting, just hands and eye.

MAJID KHAN to Glamorgan team-mates, **1969**.

I hear a lot about this wonderful footwork, but they never seem to go forward – they're always crawling backwards.

LIONEL PALAIRET on the England batsmen's difficulties with Warwick Armstrong, **1920/21**.

When you are in all day the bat never feels heavy. It is only when you are in and out quickly that it weighs.

COLIN COWDREY.

The slow and varied pace of wickets and outfielding may have had something to do with much of the bad running between the wickets seen nowadays. The two most prevalent reasons seem to be: failure of the non-batsman in backing up directly the ball leaves the bowler's hand, and bad calling. There is no excuse for either failing. They result from thoughtlessness, selfishness, laziness and ignorance, none of which should be tolerated by any real cricketer.

The Cricketer, **1924**.

When I'm coming, I say 'Yes', and when I'm not, I say 'No'.

WILFRED RHODES, explaining the secret of his excellent understanding over short singles with Jack Hobbs.

Each involved that most poignant and farcical of all cricketing situations, the sequence of call, counter-call, check and counter-check, followed by a wild scamper bringing both batsmen to the same end. No player, however impassive and well disciplined, can completely conceal the disgust and resentment which boil in the heart of one who is the victim of such an antic.

J. G. W. DAVIES on Combined Services' 1st inning's 4 run outs v Cambridge University, **1960**.

It is possible that in these days of greater reliance on push-button devices, the principles of fire and movement are not as firmly instilled into our warriors as in bygone days.

J. G. W. DAVIES, as above.

SAM COOK (during one of many running mix-ups): Call, Bomber!
'BOMBER' WELLS (his Gloucestershire team-mate): Heads!

Let's cut out some of the quick singles.
OK, Ken, we'll cut out yours.

Exchange between KEN BARRINGTON and FRED TITMUS towards end of a hot day in Australia.

His record, take it all in all,
Was not a very great one;
He seldom hit a crooked ball
And never stopped a straight one.

The Rabbit (anon).

You've got more bloody edges than a broken pisspot.

FRED TRUEMAN to Northants batsman, **1956**.

What looks smashing in the text-book isn't necessarily any good
in modern first-class cricket. Frankly my main concern as a
professional cricketer is not to look beautiful but to get runs.

KEN BARRINGTON, **1963**.

I never wanted to make a hundred. Who wants to make a hundred
anyway? When I first went in, my immediate objective was to hit
the ball to each of the four corners of the field. After that I tried
not to be repetitive.

SIR LEARIE CONSTANTINE, speech to Royal Commonwealth Society, **1963**.

Why, our incomparable Hobbs has often been very slow off the
mark . . . and has got over his bad time and helped himself to a
century.

D. J. KNIGHT (Surrey, England), advising patience in his advice to young batsmen.

I hate defensive strokes – you only get three off them.

W. G. GRACE.

Every ball was labelled: either 1, 2, 3, 4, or 6. I leave out the 5.
Too damn far to run.

CHARLIE MACARTNEY, from *Fingleton On Cricket*, **1972**.

REG DUFF (Australian batsman): You've only got one stroke,
Wilfred.
WILFRED RHODES: Aye, that's all I needed on that wicket.

Rhodes, scoring half-century in MCC's 456, Australian tour, Sydney, **1908**.

On the leg-side of the wicket lay safety; on the off the surgery windows. Small wonder, therefore, if a pronounced penchant for the 'pull' should have affected my batting throughout my days.

G. L. JESSOP on cricket at home in a small garden with attendant punishment for breaking his father's windows.

The cover drive is the most beautiful stroke in batsmanship. Does that throw any light on why I am a self-admitted lover of all things British and traditional?

COLIN COWDREY, in *MCC*, **1976**.

The cut was never a business stroke.

WILFRED RHODES.

When next I come to play against the Gentlemen of Lincolnshire I shall bring a broom-handle.

W. G. GRACE replying to a post-match toast at Grimsby. He had scored his regular hundred after apparently being out first ball.

Fender . . . gave some amusement by hitting Armstrong back-handed on the off-side for a couple.

PELHAM WARNER reporting in *The Cricketer*, England v Australia, Old Trafford, **1921**. The first reverse sweep?

It's always a good idea to aim the first ball right here at the bowler's head. They don't like it. It rattles 'em.

CHARLIE MACARTNEY, from *Fingleton On Cricket*, **1972**.

It was a hard, slow, rather dispiriting road, and for a long time the swinging ball filled me with the fear of God.

COLIN COWDREY on his early days with Kent.

A yorker, sir? I don't know. I never had one.

W. G. GRACE when asked for advice on playing yorkers.

I thought if I didn't go in tonight I'd never get in at all against that bowling.

GRACE'S explanation for not sending in a night-watchman in difficult conditions.

I thought if I wasn't good enough to bat for quarter of an hour tonight, I wasn't good enough to bat at all tomorrow.

E. R. (ROCKLEY) WILSON'S explanation in similar circumstances.

You never intimidate a good player.

GREG CHAPPELL, in *Howzat*, **1980**.

None of us likes it (fast bowling) but some of us don't let on.

MAURICE LEYLAND, England and Yorkshire batsman.

Go easy on me, young fellow, I'm getting on and you might hit me.

PATSY HENDREN'S 'con' to young paceman Alf Gover at Lord's, **1928**. (He hooked two of his first three balls for boundaries.)

Good Lord, he's knocked old George off his horse now.

GEOFF ARNOLD, watching from England's dressing room, as Dennis Lillee hit Keith Fletcher on touring cap, MCC in Australia, **1974/5**.

No good hitting me there mate, nothing to damage.

DEREK RANDALL, responding to being 'skulled' by Dennis Lillee in Centenary Test, Melbourne, **1977**.

Dear Mum, things are looking up. Today I got a half-volley in the nets.

DAVID LLOYD, Lancashire batsman, in letter home during Australian tour, **1972/3**.

Truly, I think I could get more runs if England had some faster bowlers.

VIV RICHARDS, **1976**.

Johnnie, if you ever get hit again, make sure you drop inside the crease.

BRIAN CLOSE, advice to John Hampshire, after he was poleaxed by a bouncer from Charlie Griffiths which gave him headaches for life, **1963**.

It should be a cause of real concern to administrators that the batsman himself has become as much a target as the wickets he defends.

Wisden, editorial, **1985**.

Do you wish to prefer charges?

Police sergeant to Sri Lanka's Sunil Wettimuny, when he arrived bruised in hospital during World Cup, saying that 'Jeff Thomson did it', **1975**.

Is this a time for heroics or should we go off?
I'd eff off if I were you!

Exchange between JOHN BARCLAY and JEFF THOMSON after Thomson had hit Barclay on the helmet with a bouncer.

I don't know why they bother to put the stumps out. None of those buggers are trying to hit them.

GRAEME FOWLER after an uncomfortable two hours v West Indies, Oval Test, **1985**.

I'm quite prepared to be hit. If they want to hit me, then they're going to have to keep on hitting me, because I won't give up.

DAVID SMITH, Worcestershire batsman, before West Indies tour, **1985**.

When you're both a batter and a bowler you enjoy yourself twice as much.

GEORGE HIRST.

I always maintain it is time enough to get runs when the bell is round your throat on a little blue or pink ribbon, which means you have become a rabbit as far as your bowling is concerned.

SAMMY WOODS.

I used to get bored with batting. All I ever wanted to do was bowl. I had one shot – the slog – and if I hit it, the ball went a long way and the crowd and I were happy. If I missed it, well I was that much closer to bowling.

'BOMBER' WELLS, Gloucestershire and Nottinghamshire off-spinner, in *The Spinner's Turn*, **1982**.

> . . . at last
> the bowler flails once more,
> a final twitch for the dying day.

JOHN SNOW, from *Moments and Thoughts*, **1973**.

The bowler must never be wishing to pick up any quarrel with the umpire of the opposite party.

MOHUMMUD ABDULLAH KHAN, *Introduction to Cricket Guide*, Lucknow, **1891**.

By and large cricket is governed by a self-perpetuating oligarchy of willow wielders! On almost every committee and at most conferences batters comfortably outnumber the game's honest toilers!

ROBIN MARLAR, **1959**.

The last bowler to be knighted was Sir Francis Drake.

ARTHUR MAILEY.

Bowling is just as artistic as many of the so-called higher arts, and a great deal more manly and healthy, and therefore should be treated much more seriously than it is by the average amateur.

F. R. SPOFFORTH.

There is hardly one first-class amateur bowler in England, and in my opinion, laziness is one of the main causes of this, and another is the employment of professionals at schools and universities. I have never heard an amateur say 'I am going to have a bowl', it is always a 'knock'.

F. R. SPOFFORTH, **1906**.

No bowler could call himself a bowler unless he could bowl for two hours at a stretch.

ALFRED SHAW.

For myself I should like 100 balls in the over.

ALFRED MYNN, the Lion of Kent, on the proposal to increase the over from 4 balls to 6.

County bowlers are nothing if not philosophical. I'll be there in midsummer, running up to Sir Geoffrey, convincing myself he's going to pad up to a straight one.

BRIAN BRAIN (Worcestershire, Gloucestershire), **1980**.

I became a bowler at school in the best of all possible ways – I used to bowl out the captain at the nets.

A. A. MILNE.

Bowling which does not get men out, like batting which brings no runs to the score, is an art abused.

A. E. KNIGHT, *The Complete Cricketer*, **1906**.

I wish I could watch it again and again for ever.

STUART WILKINSON, on bowling Geoffrey Boycott for 12 during Durham's defeat of Yorkshire in Gillette Cup, **1973**.

There's more in bowling than just turning your arm over. There's such a thing as observation.

WILFRED RHODES.

I suppose if I was to think every ball, they'd never get a run.

WILLIAM LILLYWHITE.

A straight ball has a certain lethal quality about it. If you miss it, you've 'ad it.

JIM SIMS (quoted in Mike Brearley, *The Art of Captaincy*, **1985**).

What they failed to say was that six of them long-'ops were straight long-'ops.

SIMS's response to an *Evening Standard* report that he had taken 8 wickets for Middlesex v Sussex with long-hops.

I can keep them there, or thereabouts.

WILFRED RHODES, then a Test selector at 48, agreeing he could still bowl a length in response to suggestions that he should be recalled against Australia in 1926. He was, taking 2–25 and 4–44, England winning by 289 runs..

Now you can start learning summat about the game.

EMMOTT ROBINSON to Yorkshire colleague Bill Bowes upon receiving his cap, **1930**.

Bill, get a notebook. Put down everything you learn about the batsmen, the way they play, their best shots, their weakest shots. For ten years you'll learn something new every day. After that you'll remember something you've forgotten.

EMMOTT ROBINSON to the young Bill Bowes.

I never bowled at the wickets: I bowled at the stroke. I intended the batsman to make a stroke, then I tried to beat it. I tried to make the batsman move. The time a batsman makes mistakes is when he has to move his feet.

SYDNEY BARNES, **1953**.

I am not unhappy to be hit for six sixes. I want batsmen to play shots. Only then can I get them out.

BISHEN BEDI.

Deliveries which batsmen play and miss at outside the off-stump when Richie Benaud is commentating.

VIC MARKS's definition of a leg-cutter, *Somerset Handbook*, **1980**.

Already the press are lamenting on the paucity of new faces among the bowling fraternity. Any wonder, what youngster in his right mind gladly looks forward to a life of little glamour, few rewards and days of being just 'cannon-fodder' for opposing batsmen?

PETER WALKER on the 1958/62, experiment with covered wickets.

What the legislators failed to take into account was that the average county player just has not the ability to surmount the precision short of a length delivery that has been the logical professional bowlers' reply to this attempt to 'process' him out of the game.

PETER WALKER on why covered wickets had not improved stroke-making.

After I've retired they should open the pitches to the elements.

PETER ROEBUCK, Somerset batsman, **1985**.

When there's a hosepipe ban covering three-quarters of the country, you don't expect a damp wicket at Lord's.

BOB WILLIS, Warwickshire's captain, after his county's loss in Benson and Hedges Cup Final against Lancashire, **1984**.

The first victim was hit on the thumb and was led out bleeding profusely, his colleague fainted and the next man in decided not to bat.

History of Radley College, on W. E. W. Collins's feat of getting three batsmen with one delivery in the 1860s.

The practice of fast bowling in our schools and colleges is sadly, almost cruelly, neglected.

LILLYWHITES's article entitled 'The Decline of Fast Bowling', **1882**.

To bowl fast is to revel in the glad animal action, to thrill in physical power and to enjoy a certain sneaking feeling of superiority over the mortals who play the game.

FRANK TYSON in *A Typhoon Called Tyson*.

The thicker you are, the better your chances of becoming a good quick bowler.

STEWART STOREY, Surrey coach, in *From The Nursery End*, **1985**.

Maturity brings cunning to the fast bowler and adds yet another facet to his nature, other modes of attack to his repertoire. Yet the coming of guile to quick bowling can be like the advance of creeping paralysis to the body.

FRANK TYSON.

Outwardly, thought and cunning methods add to the armoury of the quick bowler and make him the complete, shrewd, mechanically perfect athlete. Inwardly, guile saps the psychological foundations of the edifice of fast bowling until it takes away the real desire and very reasons for wanting to bowl quick.

FRANK TYSON.

There's no sitting duck like a scared duck.

RAY LINDWALL.

Speaking as a one-time fast bowler, who was also on the distinctly short side of length, it does not take one long to spot the player . . . who is always fearing the worst. A fast bowler, when he has gained this unsettling influence, can scarcely be blamed if he plays up to it.

G. L. JESSOP.

When (William) Barnes came into bat, W.G., who wasn't captain
. . . said to me 'keep em short'. I did and hit Barnes over the
heart first ball. I think he got a two and then out. In the second
innings I again kept them short and again hit him in the ribs. I
apologised.

S. M. J. WOODS.

Sorry Doc, she slipped.

ERNEST JONES, Australian fast bowler, firing delivery through W. G. Grace's
beard during rout of England, **1896**.

I used to give every new batsman four balls. One was a bouncer
to check his courage, the second a fizzer to check his eyesight,
the third was a slow-un to try out his reflexes and the fourth a
bender to see if he was a good cricketer. And if he took a single
of each of the four balls, I knew I was in trouble.

HAROLD LARWOOD, **1972**.

Remember lad, one day we'll have a fast bowler – and I hope
that day isn't far off.

LEN HUTTON to Ray Lindwall after some torrid overs, **1950/51**.

I shouldn't have done that.

RAY LINDWALL upon hitting Tyson with a bouncer during the Australia v England
series, **1954/5**.

I wanted to show him how fast I was.

RAY LINDWALL's later explanation for hitting Tyson.

I want to hit you Bailey – I want to hit you over the heart.

South African pace bowler PETER HEINE to Trevor Bailey.

When tha's laikin' wi Fred, tha's not laikin' wi a soft ball, tha
knows.

FRED TRUEMAN, in *Fast Fury*, **1961**.

I try to hit a batsman in the rib cage when I bowl a purposeful bouncer, and I want it to hurt so much that the batsman doesn't want to face me any more.

DENNIS LILLEE, *Back To The Mark*, **1974**.

I enjoy hitting a batsman more than getting him out. I like to see blood on the pitch. And I've been training on whisky.

JEFF THOMSON, **1974**.

I know I'm a ruthless bastard and I'll always have a go. But I wouldn't deliberately put a ball like that on anybody. It slipped. It honestly slipped.

DENNIS LILLEE, after beamer to Bob Willis in Sydney, Australia v MCC, **1974/5** tour.

When I hear Colin bowl de bounces, I get vex. Two bounces an over okay, but when he bowl five I get vex bad. I tell him, what happen if he hit batsmen and he fall dead on de spot?

Colin Croft's mother, during England's tour of West Indies, **1981** (from *Cricket Wallah*, Scyld Berry, 1982).

I don't want any bloody sympathy, do you understand that? It has happened. People who say 'I know how you feel' are just talking bullshit. They don't know, not at all. What I can't forget is that the ball was a deliberate short one. Not deliberately at his head, but still deliberate.

PETER LEVER, after felling Ewen Chatfield, New Zealand's No. 11, with a short delivery, Auckland Test **1975**. Chatfield was hit on the temple and his heart stopped for several seconds.

You look a sight worse than I do.

EWEN CHATFIELD, when Lever visited him in Auckland hospital, **1975**.

Remember, with these speedsters bowling at 95 miles per hour, cricket can kill.

Australian TV advert for Packer circus, **1977**.

England's pace bowlers are making the helmet go out of fashion.

SCYLD BERRY, the *Observer*, **1981**.

If you have guys who are going to stay around and be stubborn, and obviously make fast bowlers look like they are not fast bowlers, I can't see why they shouldn't be softened up a bit.

VIV RICHARDS replying to **1985** *Wisden's* criticism of Marshall's bowling at Pocock the previous summer.

This is our weapon now, so we have got to use it.

VIV RICHARDS on West Indies' possession of a powerful speed attack.

I have never felt it more likely that we should see someone killed.

JOHN WOODCOCK, in *The Times*, following England's mauling by West Indies pace bowlers, Kingston Test, **1986**.

The retaliation is simple and straightforward. Having successfully(?) evaded the head-high bouncer the batsman should feel entitled to straighten up, go into a hammer-thrower's crouch and hurl his bat at the bowler just completing his follow through. This to me sounds fair game.

PETER WALKER'S suggestion for countering the proliferation of bouncers, **1962**.

As I grew older, the elastic snapped. I lost the pace, the zip and the sting had gone. I remember taking two catches off my own bowling against Glamorgan and being complimented on my cleverly disguised slower ball.

TED DEXTER, *Wisden Cricket Monthly*, **1980**.

That season (1897) was the first in which the idea that the ball could be made to swing in the air appeared to us as a workable proposition.

G. L. JESSOP.

Keep your arm up, Fred.

W. G. GRACE's admonition to Roberts when the Gloucestershire seamer
experimented swinging the ball by bowling round arm.

The frequent adjurations to 'Keep your arm up, Fred' had rather
a dampening influence on his effectiveness.

G. L. JESSOP on Grace's failure to encourage Gloucestershire seamer Fred Roberts
attempts to swing the ball by bowling round-arm.

The batsman knows that medium-pace bowlers won't become
'quick' by suddenly acquiring a 'drag' and start assaulting him
from about 18 yards.

PETER RICHARDSON on the new front foot no-ball rule, 1963.

Before the season began a great deal was heard of how bowlers
were having to completely alter their actions and run-ups, and
how it was almost certain to bring about the death of all genuine
fast bowlers. We now know it has driven no-one out of the game.

PETER RICHARDSON.

Throughout English cricket the seam bowler rides high and the
spinner sinks further into oblivion. We must be concerned with
this trend and we would be neglecting our duty to ignore it.

S. C. GRIFFITH, MCC Secretary, in his annual speech to County Secretaries, 1963.

I shall bowl the first ball but I don't know about a full over. I
can't really spin 'em now. I can cut 'em, of course, but any fool
can do that.

SYDNEY BARNES, bowling first over of match to mark his 80th birthday, Barnes's
XI v England XI, 1953.

If I came into the game now, I'd probably end up as a medium-
pace dobber.

FRED TITMUS, former England off-spinner, 1982.

The mentality of the medium-pace bowler as a general rule does not rate up to that of the more subtle type of bowler.

ARTHUR MAILEY.

With very few exceptions the great spin bowlers of cricket were personalities and men of character – not always pleasant but invariably interesting. They may have lacked the charm and friendliness of their faster confederates; they may have been more temperamental and less self-disciplined; but there seemed to be an absence of orthodoxy about them and they were able to meander through life as individuals not as civil servants.

ARTHUR MAILEY.

Slow bowling is an art, Mr Kelly, and art is international.

ARTHUR MAILEY replying to a reprimand from the Australian manager for giving advice to England leg-break bowler Ian Peebles on the **1930** Tour, Manchester Test.

When a spinner comes on, your eyes go round like dollar signs on a fruit machine. Everyone wants to hit him because they can't smash the fast bowler.

ALLAN LAMB, England batsman, **1982**.

One general and melancholy fact may indeed be noticed here. No less than five of the six leading counties have found it necessary to begin their attack with slow bowlers . . . The causes of this dreary and monotonous prevalence of slow bowling are many and amongst the most noteworthy may be cited the extraordinary and exaggerated excellence of grounds, the immense number of first-class matches which the increased facilities of locomotion have brought into existence and, lastly, the absolute mastery which, for five or six years, Mr W. G. Grace acquired over fast bowling.

Lillywhite's Cricketers' Companion, about **1880** season.

It's all a matter of inches – those between your ears.

ARTHUR MILTON, on spin bowling, **1982**.

The great thing about spin bowling is that it is an art which can be learnt. In that sense it is different from fast bowling. A fast bowler either has the natural ability to hurl the ball down quickly or he hasn't. And if he can't do it, there is no way you can coach it into him. The reverse is true of spin bowling. I believe you can learn it from scratch.

RAY ILLINGWORTH, in *Spin Bowling*, **1980**.

If a batsman thinks it's spinning, then it's spinning.

WILFRED RHODES (quoted in Neville Cardus, *Autobiography*, **1947**).

It's all tommy-rot this talk about dropping a ball on a sixpence. Let 'em try and hit a kitchen hearth-rug.

TED PEATE, Yorkshire slow left armer, **1880s**, whose accuracy was legendary.

Try the morning paper.

WILFRED RHODES's gloss on Peate's statement.

The googly, thank heaven, was unknown in those good days. A captain could place his fieldsmen to accurate bowling, and a batsman knew which way the ball was going to break, enabling him to adopt the right position to deal with every honest trick of the bowler. Today all this is changed, and one becomes nauseated with the frequency with which colossal scores are made, and the rapidity of the batsmen would satisfy even a New York baseball crowd.

A. C. MACLAREN on the effects of the googly bowler, **1921**.

It must be very humiliating for any skipper to see balls bouncing twice, with full pitches and long hops thrown in as a matter of course.

A. C. MACLAREN on googly bowling.

I hope the day will come when the bowler will be no-balled whenever he sends down an illegitimate break.

A. C. MACLAREN.

It was rather a pity Ellis got run out at 1,107, because I was just striking a length.

ARTHUR MAILEY after taking 4–362 while Victoria scored 1,107 v New South Wales, **1926**.

Very few chances were given, but I think a chap in a tweed coat dropped Jack Ryder (295) near the shilling stand.

ARTHUR MAILEY on Victoria's 1,107 v New South Wales, **1926**.

In 1949, the decree went out that county groundsmen should strive to prepare more sporting wickets, in the belief that the *shirt-front* type of wicket was responsible for much of the dull cricket of the day. Little did people realise that this decision was to be the death-knell of the wrist-spinner, who must always be more expensive than the good finger spinner.

COLIN COWDREY, *The Cricketer*, **1963**.

I remember playing in dozens of matches with Douglas Wright when he should never have been in the side. Not only did we find ourselves playing with ten men, but with every over of honest toil he was driving another nail into our own coffin.

COLIN COWDREY.

Gentlemen, I think you might put me in on Monday morning and get me out by about Saturday night.

FULLER PILCH, asked his opinion of underhand bowling, **1820s**.

When I've bowled the ball, I've done with her and leaves her to my field.

WILLIAM LILLYWHITE.

Ye Wicket Keepers shall stand at a reasonable distance behind ye Wicket, and shall not move till ye Ball is out of ye Bowlers hand, and shall not by any noise incommode ye Striker, and if his hands, knees foot or head be over before ye Wicket, though ye Ball hit it, it shall not be Out.

Law for Wicket Keepers, **1744**.

It can therefore be laid down as an absolute principle in team selection that the best wicket-keeper, irrespective of all other considerations, should always be chosen.

MCC Coaching Manual.

I should like this man to be of a grave demeanour and humble mind.

MOHUMMUD ABDULLAH KHAN on wicket-keepers, *Introduction to Cricket Guide*, **1891**.

You must rinse your hands in the chamberpot every day. The urine hardens them wonderfully.

HERBERT STRUDWICK, the former England wicket-keeper, offering advice to A. G. Pawson of Oxford University.

I shall have to catch a later train tonight – that one knocked off the 7.30.

FRED STEDMAN, predecessor of Strudwick as Surrey wicket-keeper, who used a copy of the South Western railway timetable as protection, after he was hit in chest.

There are three reasons I can be wicket-keeping badly . . . lack of concentration, standing up too soon, or snatching at the ball. The longer you stay crouching, even for a thousandth of a second, may mean the difference between the ball glancing off your finger or sticking to the middle of your glove.

BOB TAYLOR.

A wicket-keeper who is on his toes is likely to overbalance.

C. B. PONSONBY (Worcestershire, **1920s**).

A slack, careless fielder needs the stick: he cannot possibly have a right and proper spirit.

RANJITSINHJI, *The Jubilee Book Of Cricket*, **1897**.

I just put my hand down as a pretence, which pleases the crowd, taking good care never to touch the ball, which pleases me, and so everybody is satisfied.

GEORGE GIFFEN (South Australia) giving advice to Charles McLeod (Victoria) after the latter had injured himself stopping Giffen's fierce straight drive.

The fielders must take especial care not to exchange jokes with one another, or try funny tricks, that do secretly divide their attention and produce a horrible defect in their fielding.

MOHUMMUD ABDULLAH KHAN, *Introduction to Cricket Guide*, **1891**.

(Point) must be a very smart and clever man, of a quick sight and slender form; pay great attention to the game my dear pointer or suppose yourself already hurt.

MOHUMMUD ABDULLAH KHAN, *Introduction to Cricket Guide*, **1891**.

I only just have to perch myself at short leg and just stare at some of 'em to get 'em out. They fiddle about and look away and then they look back to see if I'm staring at 'em. I am. They don't stay long.

BRIAN CLOSE.

Thee get on with thi lakin', and I'll get on wi' mine.

EMMOTT ROBINSON, of Yorkshire, warned he was in danger fielding close to bat.

Be ready for rebounds!

BRIAN CLOSE (short square) to Ray East (forward short leg).

The only thing which I'm very keen to do before I leave Somerset is to throw myself at the ball, and to dive, as I see the other team-mates in the Somerset team do. And I'm sure when I do, when I really do dive, I'm going to get a big applause.

SUNIL GAVASKAR, BBC Eastern Service, **1980**.

There's an epidemic around here, but it isn't catching.

TOM EMMETT suffering a spate of dropped catches.

After working all day I just go down to the river and catch the swallows as they flit by.

G. J. BONNOR (Australia) explaining his ability as a slip. Sammy Woods said he didn't believe the yarn, but he added that Bonnor, who was 6'5", 'had very long arms'.

Short boundaries, by decreasing the opportunities for good fielding, rob cricket of half its charm.

Wisden, editorial, **1906**.

When I went to find out what all the fuss was about I found several people trampling around my garden looking for the ball.

TONY MARTIN, resident of Park Road, Dartford, bombarded during Clive Lloyd's 163 for Lancashire v Kent, **1970**.

A coach who suppresses natural instincts may find that he has lifted a poor player to a mediocre one but has reduced a potential genius to the rank and file.

SIR DON BRADMAN, **1967**.

If style counts for anything (and who really would attempt to deny it?), it simply must be insisted upon; in which case, in nine instances out of ten – bang goes individualism.

MAJOR G. A. FAULKNER, South African player and cricket coach. *The Cricketer*, **1925**.

I find it mystifying that England produces any cricketers at all.

COLIN MCCOOL on English coaching.

I was never coached; I was never told how to hold a bat.

SIR DON BRADMAN.

I've lost more good players through interfering parents than for any other reason.

COLIN PAGE, Kent coach, in *From The Nursery End*, **1985**.

There is an accent on sameness in approach, sameness in method, none of which helps to make the game more eye-catching. This uniformity has extended itself into wearing apparel – a coloured cap is looked upon as definitely 'Non-U' among professionals – and in batting styles. Numbers one to eight are carbon copies of each other both in technique and tactical approach.

PETER WALKER in *The Cricketer*, **1963**.

In these degenerate days, when even youngsters at school and 'varsity go in to bat on perfect pitches against nothing faster than medium-paced deliveries wearing strange pads, one's thoughts instinctively turn to the days of fiery wickets and genuine fast bowlers.

R. O. EDWARDS, *The Cricketer*, **1921**.

With regard to the pernicious habit of getting in front of the wicket, as many of our best batsmen do when playing a straight ball, there is only one way to stop that, and that is by prohibiting pads, except little shinguards as used in football. Batsmen would soon give up playing the ball with their legs like Shrewsbury, Gunn and Co. used to in the old days.

C. I. THORNTON, *The Cricketer*, **1921**.

No boy will ever have any chance of becoming a batsman if he is not taught to wear leg-guards and batting gloves. If he is provided with these there is no excuse for stepping to leg, which is 'bad form' and does not tend to increase the prestige of an XI.

E. A. HUMPHREY PENN, 'Common Faults in Schoolboy Cricket', *The Cricketer*, **1927**.

It is ghastly to have to keep bending your head down to adjust a defective buckle, especially on a hot day. The blood rushes to your head, and you get up and face the bowling with the most hopelessly dizzy feeling . . .

D. J. KNIGHT, 'Advice on Batsmanship', *The Cricketer*, **1921**.

Batting gloves are candidly a nuisance, but they must always be worn on both hands, and the temptation to tear them off and fling them to the square-leg umpire must be fought most strenuously.

D. J. KNIGHT.

There was a young fresher called Jessop
Who was pitching 'em less up and less up,
'Til one of the pros,
Got a blow on the nose
And said: 'In a helmet I'll dress up.'

Early reference to use of batting helmets, Cambridge University limerick, after Gilbert Jessop bowled bumpers, 'varsity match, **1896**.

I don't know what the game's coming to. You wouldn't get me wearing one of those plastic things.

BRIAN CLOSE, on Tony Cordle's use of a fielding helmet for Glamorgan, following near-fatal injury to his team-mate Roger Davis, **1971**.

The increased weights of bats has contributed to our weakness in hooking. The shot demands speed of stroke and timing. How much simpler it is to swat a fly with a rolled up newspaper than with a telephone directory.

DENIS COMPTON, in *Cricket And All That*, **1978**.

I wore a shilling cap, a sixpenny belt with a snake-clasp and brown boots. At the trial I bowled in my sweater, but I was better off than Arthur Mold of Lancashire, who couldn't take his off because he had no shirt on underneath. My shirt was blue, but I got a white one with my first money . . .

GEORGE HIRST on his trial for Yorkshire, **1889**.

A boy should wear boots for cricket. He can neither bat, bowl nor field well in shoes. If he cannot afford cricket boots he should be allowed to wear football boots. Not very elegant, but safe and conducive to better play.

HUMPHREY PENN, *The Cricketer*, **1927**.

On the second day of the match, just after lunch, a certain bowler's waistband went with a pop in mid-delivery of a length ball, thus occasioning an appeal for caught at the wicket. Furthermore Frances Browne so far failed to preserve the aesthetic unities of the game by bowling in what seemed to be light blue rope-soled shoes.

R. C. ROBERTSON-GLASGOW, All Gibralter v Cryptics, **1927**; from *The Cricketer*.

It is a good thing to carry a scarf to put round the neck between innings. It looks smart – and there is no harm in doing your side credit – and cools one off gradually.

CROSS-ARROW, *The Cricketer*, **1927**.

If you like a white sun hat always carry one with you. C. B. Fry played some of his greatest innings in a sun hat.

CROSS-ARROW, *The Cricketer*, **1927**.

I'm going to make them wear their caps this season. After all, you don't get awarded your county floppy hat, do you?

JACK BOND, Lancashire CCC manager, **1985**.

We had different ideas of fitness. To me the best preparation for batting, bowling and fielding was batting, bowling and fielding. I doubt if many of my contemporaries, especially the older ones, did many exercises. I have often tried to picture Evans and Compton doing press-ups in the outfield before the day's play but so far have failed miserably.

PETER MAY, chairman of Test selectors, in *A Game Enjoyed*, **1985**.

If I want to get fit for bowling, I do a lot of bowling.

BRIAN STATHAM, Lancashire and England, **1974**.

We are fitter than any side I have ever known at Yorkshire.

DAVID BAIRSTOW after the county's pre-season training at Catterick Army camp, **1985**.

New Ball Pair No. 14.

Yorkshire Post headline on the Yorkshire bowlers' injury problems, **1985**.

I'm resigned to the fact that I may end up in a wheelchair any time.

GRAHAM DILLEY, Kent pace bowler, returning after neck operation, **1985**.

During the winter I train on 20 fags and a couple of pints a lager and a prolonged diet of cricket talk.

BRIAN BRAIN, Gloucestershire seamer, *Another Day, Another Match*, **1981**.

I absolutely insist that all my boys should be in bed before breakfast.

COLIN INGLEBY-MACKENZIE, explaining reason for Hampshire's success under his captaincy, on BBC Radio, **1960s**.

If these young men think they can field out all day, on such a day as Thursday was, dance all night at the Hawks ball (which they were practically compelled to attend) and then do themselves justice with the bat the next morning, then they are very much mistaken.

'Cantab' on Cambridge University cricket in *The Cricketer*, **1925**.

Sleep is essential, especially during the cricket season; we would place 8 hours as an absolute minimum; ten is better still. Smoking is bad, especially cigarettes, and, of course, excess in eating and drinking is still worse. Reading late at night, too, spells ruin for the eyes.

D. J. KNIGHT – first axiom of batsmanship – good health.

Vegetarianism may be a cure for all the ills which flesh is heir to, but it is wretched stuff to make runs on. For the whole month of May I could get neither runs nor wickets.

G. L. JESSOP on his poor form in May **1898**, after an attack of renal colic.

The 'Old Man' (W.G.) was much concerned over my ill success, and resolved to prescribe for me in his own fashion. I forget whether it was Goelet 1889, or Moet 1886 . . . anyway it had the desired effect, and I bade farewell to vegetarianism for ever.

G. L. JESSOP on his return to form.

Hey, Greigy. This champagne's alright, but the blackcurrant jam tastes of fish.

DEREK RANDALL, sampling caviar on MCC tour to India, **1976/7**.

But, beggin' your lordships' pardons, it strikes me as bein' like this, beggin' your lordships' pardons – if Ah can go down to Lord's and get drunk and mek a century 'fore lunch, then Ah thinks it ud pay t'Notts Committee to get mi drunk afore every match.

BILLY BARNES, reprimanded by Nottinghamshire committee, after arriving late and drunk – but still scoring a century against Middlesex at Lord's (from Neville Cardus's *Autobiography*, **1947**).

Kids in the West feel a bit peckish and buy a carton of junk-food. Plenty here can't afford to do that. So they have to eat lots of fruit and other good wholesome grub that happens to be the cheapest and the best for them. Add all the bits and pieces together and you get a long, long queue of fit, lean, loose-moving youngsters who are superbly fitted to the job.

ARTHUR WAIGHT, West Indies physio, explaining the West Indies surfeit of fast bowlers in the **1980s**.

We used to eat so many salads, there was a danger of contracting myxomatosis.

RAY EAST, describing lunchtime offerings on the county circuit, in *A Funny Turn*, **1983**.

You can't consider yourself a County Cricketer until you've eaten a ton and a half of lettuce.

GARY SOBERS welcoming West Indian newcomer to the circuit.

I always have my lunch at 1.30 pm.

GEORGE GUNN, Nottinghamshire batsman, deliberately giving his wicket away after learning lunch interval was later than usual.

It seems to me the tea interval is an unnecessary evil. Why should there be a tea interval in Saturday afternoon cricket? It is an old-fashioned institution . . . Surely it is not necessary that a team must all sit down to tea together like a school treat.

A. W. T. LANGFORD, 'Club Cricket' in *The Cricketer*, **1928**.

Thorough sportsmen they were and men who made a day of a match on Saturday. Where we went to play, there we dined. Not like the present club cricket, 'When is the next train home?'

S. M. J. WOODS (Somerset, England) comparing club cricket in the **1890s** and **1923**.

There is a lot of cricket spirit and cricket philosophy in that statement 'where we played, there we dined'.

LAURENCE WOODHOUSE, 'Ruminations' in *The Cricketer*, **1923**.

Most county cricketers play the game for the life rather than the living. For them it's the motorways of England rather than the jet lanes of the world. It's sausage, egg and chips at Watford Gap rather than vol-au-vent and small talk on the Governor-General's lawns in Barbados.

MICHAEL CAREY.

The objection (to longer hours of play on the 3rd day) will be raised that the train service does not suit. How often nowadays do you read of a match being stopped at 5.30 pm to enable Blankshire to catch their train? It was not ever thus. Many and many a night have I spent in a train moving from ground to ground.

FRANK MITCHELL, *The Cricketer*, **1927**.

I could a bowt t'taxi for less.

ARTHUR WOOD, Yorkshire wicket-keeper, after rushing by taxi from Scarborough for Test début v Australians at Lord's, **1938**.

It is a mistake to think that the game as it is played now is a super physical strain. The comforts are greater – hotels and travelling – the pay is doubled, the hours are less. It is difficult to find fault with a life so pleasant as is that of the county cricketer.

The Cricketer, **1931**.

A whole generation of professional cricketers has emerged who don't know the sheer pleasure of lazing around on a free Sunday . . . the Saturday nights when you didn't have to climb into the car and drive 150 miles after a long day in the field. You could have a few pints with the opposition, a night on the town and then relax next morning in bed with the Sunday papers, contemplating nothing more strenuous than a game of golf in the afternoon.

BRIAN BRAIN, *Another Day, Another Match*, **1981**.

Football managers don't look on county cricketers as professionals, but just because they enjoy themselves they are no less professional. There is more comradeship in cricket and nowhere near so much back-stabbing as in football. Cricketers always accept defeat, footballers cannot.

JIM CUMBES, Aston Villa and Worcestershire, **1975**.

The wheels of the social bandwagon have come off. The five cans of ale that the old-timers might have enjoyed before a civilised dinner each night have turned into prolonged, boredom drinking in public.

BOB WILLIS, *Lasting The Pace*, **1985**.

I have been to many functions where some of the great cricketers of the past have been present . . . To see some of them sink their drink is to witness performances as awe-inspiring as ever any of them displayed on the cricket field.

IAN BOTHAM, excusing use of marijuana, **1986**.

By! This is real!

BARRY WOOD's reaction to social life on the county circuit, **1964**.

In international cricket a player should be made to fight for everything he gets on the field in gratitude for all the things he gets for nothing off the field.

ARTHUR MAILEY.

Behind the façade of the Test class player and the glamour attributed to the International game by the press, lies Mr Average county cricketer. No £500 appearance money for a series against the tourists, no overseas tours with their opportunities to broaden one's outlook and, outside of their local papers, little publicity. For most, intermixed with the outdoor life and grand fellowship that exists among the 17 counties, lies a lot of heartache, fierce disappointments, sudden elations and regular separations from their families.

PETER WALKER.

Sometimes I'm standing in the slips and I start day dreaming. I think what the hell am I doing here. What a waste of time. There must be more important things to do for a living. And sitting in the pavilion after I've been in, that's the worst of the lot. I can't stand watching cricket.

BARRY RICHARDS, 1974.

It has been suggested tonight that no-one may again do what I've been lucky enough to do this season. I don't know about that but I do know this – if he does, he'll be tired.

GEORGE HIRST, after scoring over 2,000 runs and taking more than 200 wickets for Yorkshire in a season, 1906.

If anyone beats it, they'll be bloody tired.

FRED TRUEMAN, becoming England's leading Test wicket-taker, 1964.

When Fred reached his 307 he said afterwards that anyone who passed him would be very tired. Well, you can tell him I'm not.

BOB WILLIS, becoming England's leading Test wicket-taker in New Zealand, 1984.

Towards the end of a dry season, when the nails in your boots feel as if they had been placed inside instead of outside the soles, I admit to a feeling of fatigue.

J. B. HOBBS, 1921.

All the time I keep telling myself and telling the others 'It could be worse, fellas. We could be putting a helmet on for a shift down t'pit'.

GEOFF BOYCOTT on bad days.

This miners' strike is ridiculous. There's tea ladies at the top of the mine who are earning more than county cricketers. Arthur Scargill ought to come down here and try bowling twenty overs.

RAY ILLINGWORTH, then Leicestershire captain, 1975.

It is a contrasting sign of the times that the star player is making so much money indirectly from the game that created him that unless Auntie Clara and the two poodles are allowed to tour with him, he is not disposed to represent England overseas.

WILFRED WOOLLER referring to Lock's statement that he would not be available for the **1962/3** tour of Australia unless his wife went too.

I don't care what money I get man – it's the buzz of playing for Australia that's got me.

GREG MATTHEWS, making Test debut, **1983**.

Brighter cricket, more entertaining cricket, quicker cricket, less cricket had its variant of support. But my belief is that whatever cricket reforms were instigated, they will prove no lasting panacea for financial illness . . . first class cricket will stand or fall in this decade by business foresight and planning.

WILFRED WOOLLER, **1961**.

It should surprise no-one that cricket is not self-supporting. It never has been.

COLIN COWDREY, in *MCC*, **1976**.

Cricket must be the only business where you can make more money in one day than you can in three.

PAT GIBSON, *Daily Express*, **1975**.

In recent years too many people have been concerned with what cricket could do for them rather than what they could do for cricket.

SIR DON BRADMAN, receiving life membership of Australian Cricket Society, **1984**.

The modern cricketer will do a lot for money. He will hawk autographed miniature cricket bats in Calcutta, one of the world's most impoverished cities, to children in the crowd at £15 a time.

JOHN WOODCOCK, *The Times*, **1977**.

Mr Stoddart, Mr Woods, will you please have a drink with me. I think I have enough money to pay out of my benefit.

WILLIAM BARNES (Nottinghamshire, England) after a poorly attended benefit match.

Barnes be paid 7s 6d for batting when his score reaches 50, and also 10s 6d per match for bowling when he captures six wickets per match, not unless.

S. F. BARNES's contract with Rishton, **1896**.

That no gentleman ought to make a profit by his services in the cricket field, and that for the future no cricketer who takes more than his expenses in any match shall be qualified to play for The Gentlemen against The Players at Lord's; but that if any gentleman feels difficulty in joining the match without pecuniary assistance, he shall not be debarred from playing as a Gentleman by having his actual expenses defrayed.

MCC committee resolution on amateur status, **1878**.

Cricket in London is nearly all professional; even the gentlemen make a profession of it.

REV. JAMES PYCROFT, **1851**.

One well-known cricketer in particular . . . has made larger profits by playing cricket than any professional ever made.

Shamateurism, as noted in case of W. G. Grace in *Lillywhite's Cricketers' Companion*, **1878**.

Through the spontaneous generosity of some road sweepers, who apparently rested from their labours for a short while, I was presented with a collection of 1s 5½d.

D. L. A. JEPHSON on scoring 200 for Ashley v Hornsey in **1903**. He had refused to play for Gentlemen v Players in order to play in the club match.

The committee rejected any solution of the problem on the lines of abolishing the distinction between Amateur and Professional and regarding them as 'cricketers'. They considered that the distinctive status of the amateur cricketer was not obsolete, was of great value to the game and should be preserved. The Professionals whom they had consulted supported these views.

Report of special MCC committee, chaired by Duke of Norfolk, on amateur status, **1958**.

Whilst recognising that the Amateurs were fully entitled to the repayment of genuine out-of-pocket expenses incurred while playing, and that the counties themselves must be the final judge of such claims, the committee were disturbed by the apparent over-liberal interpretation of the words 'expenses' in certain cases that had come to their notice.

As above.

I've just realised I forgot to ask the firm for leave of absence. Cricket isn't my living and I'm a bit embarrassed. I've sent off an apologetic letter of explanation.

BEV CONGDON, New Zealand captain, during tour of England, **1973**.

Some people had the idea one could go on playing cricket for ever and Oxfam would look after your children.

JOHN WARR, an amateur, retiring from Middlesex, **1967**.

It was so late in the season that some of the best amateurs were spending their holidays far away from cricket grounds and would be, of course, out of practice.

LORD HARRIS on the difficulties of recruiting the England side to play Australia at The Oval, **1880**, the first England v Australia Test.

I wrote to Mr A. G. Steel begging him to give up his shooting in Scotland for the purpose.

LORD HARRIS, as above.

Steady, Mr Christopherson, steady! I'm getting ten bob a run.

TED PEATE to Stanley Christopherson, his last wicket partner, during England v Australia Test series, **1884**.

The captain's orders had to come before Teddy Peate's ten bobs, and I was caught off a mishit next over. Peate was quite sad about it.

CHRISTOPHERSON'S account of the above incident.

In all games where there is any pecuniary benefit to be derived, the professional invariably beats the amateur, and the reason is easily found in the fact that the professional works much harder than the amateur.

F. R. SPOFFORTH in *Great Bowlers* (ed. G. W. Beldham and C. B. Fry), **1906**.

It is surprising that the general public take so little interest in the School matches at Lord's, for to the really keen cricketer they are delightful, and form a pleasant relaxation from county cricket. Moreover, one sees, let us hope, many a Gentleman of England in these games, for the Public Schools are, of course, the nurseries of amateur cricket.

PELHAM WARNER, in *The Cricketer*, **1925**.

If some of the counties in August would encourage 'varsity and public school players and give an occasional rest to a professional, they would, I am sure, benefit in the long run.

PELHAM WARNER, *The Cricketer*, **1926**.

There are many splendid young amateurs available, both at the 'varsities and in business, who are only too proud and anxious to play for their counties were the opportunity afforded them. The ideal side of any county eleven is either six amateurs and five professionals, or five amateurs and six professionals but because the northern counties have closed the door to the amateur for so many years it is quite fashionable now in the Midlands and the South to pursue the same course, in spite of the bad times and the false cry that the amateur is so unobtainable today. No more catching or untrue remark has ever perpetrated the game than the recent cry of 'Wolf' concerning the amateur.

The Cricketer, **1931**.

The end of the 1961 season has brought forth from the leading critics their annual plea for more amateurs in the game and a consequently brighter approach. They are forgetting that the game is played by a majority of professional players and that the contemporary amateur is usually as much of an employee of a county as any professional. As for an 'amateur approach', a careful study will reveal that this too is a modern myth. Today's alleged leaders in brighter cricket are often the dullest and most cautious members of their sides.

PETER WALKER, 1961.

Pray God no professional may ever captain England.

LORD HAWKE.

Amateurs always have made, and always will make, the best captains; and this is only natural.

A. G. STEEL.

T. Emmett be made captain in the absence of a gentleman.

Yorkshire committee minutes, **1878**.

There have always been disadvantages in having a professional as captain of a county team; for instance, he can be nagged at in the dressing room by his fellows, and is always liable to be a butt for grumblers, whilst he can never exercise the same authority as an amateur.

LORD HAWKE, *Recollections and Reminiscences*, **1924**.

I'm very glad we have an amateur again.

Middlesex committee man, mistakenly, to Mike Brearley on his appointment as county captain, **1971**.

Ames, I see you are wearing the county tie there. You know, don't you, that strictly speaking you are not entitled to wear it . . . I think it would be better if you didn't in future.

Kent official to Les Ames, professional, **1930s** (from *The Gloves Are Off*, Godfrey Evans, **1960**).

I shave twice a day so you can shave once.

LORD HAWKE to his Yorkshire professionals after assuming captaincy, **1883**.

I have heard some English captains speak to their professionals like dogs.

JOE DARLING, Australian captain, **1902**.

It is rather curious that the Australians themselves do not realise that our professionals prefer to be 'on their own' off the field rather than to be in the same hotel as the amateurs. Indeed, I know that some of our professionals would prefer to have second-class passages on board ship rather than having to dress each night for dinner.

LORD HAWKE.

The professional cricketer is a splendid fellow. He is loyal and steady, the best of companions on a tour, and always ready to oblige, but the amateur must be encouraged.

The Cricketer, 'Notes and Comments', **1921**.

The cricket professional is more deserving than most of those who minister to human pleasure. It is only too lamentable to think that the goal of his aspiration is, too frequently, to be the proprietor of a public house.

Leading article in *The Times*, **1882**.

The average professional cricketer is purely and simply a tradesman, and in most cases he has learnt his trade in a pretty grim school. He has a six-day-a-week job, and the regularity of his work is likely to drive him into a groove. Unless he is a very exceptional man he stays in that groove for security and the result is loss of incentive, the spirit of adventure and enterprise.

ARTHUR MAILEY.

Frank Woolley and Jack Hobbs . . . were far too modest to be anything but pros. Both were self-contained, and while their style of batting was consistent with amateurism, both realised, like the champion egg-laying hen, that if their product wasn't up to standard, the fact of wearing a crown wouldn't save their heads.

ARTHUR MAILEY.

Although Jack did have the honour of captaining England, he felt at the time like the best man who was asked to become a bigamist because the groom failed to appear.

ARTHUR MAILEY.

No games have given me more pleasure than these tussles with the professors.

G. L. JESSOP on the Gentlemen v Players matches.

I could make ducks enough at Bury St Edmunds without going up to London to make them before a crowd.

JOHN FRANCIS, Suffolk captain, explaining why he had turned down an invitation to play for Gentlemen v Players, **1870s**.

Each time I receive the invitation to play in the Gentlemen v Players match, I am as excited as a boy.

SIR JACK HOBBS near the end of his career.

The plain-spoken little bumpkin, in his eagerness and delight, and forgetting the style in which we were always accustomed to impress our aristocratic playmates with our acknowledgement of their rank and station, bawled out – 'Ah! it was *tedious* near you, Sir!' The familiarity of his tone, and the genuine Hampshire dialect in which it was spoken, set the whole ground laughing.

JOHN NYREN, *The Young Cricketer's Tutor* on Lambert, 'The Little Farmer', almost bowling the Duke of Dorset with an off-break.

High and low, rich and poor, greet one another practically on an equality, and sad will be the day for England if Socialism ever succeeds in putting class v class and thus ending sports which have made England.

LORD HAWKE, *Recollections and Reminiscences*, **1924**.

Loyalty to one's captains and one's comrades is the beginning and end of a cricketer's creed and when we find an England player so grossly infringing every rule of courtesy, common sense and discipline, it is surely time to enter the strongest possible protest.

The Cricketer on Cecil Parkin. It later described him as 'first cricketing bolshevist'. Parkin's ghosted column had criticized Gilligan's failure to bowl him v S. Africa, Edgbaston **1924**. Parkin subsequently refused to speak to his ghost again.

Bolshevism is rampant, and seeks to abolish all laws and rules, and this year cricket has not escaped its attack.

LORD HARRIS in *The Cricketer*, **1922**. Hammond chose to play for Gloucestershire rather than his native Kent.

But the second day was played under the cloud of the general strike, and since then serious cricket at Oxford has been seen no more. Legge, after covering incredible distances at illegal speeds in his Vauxhall, transporting workers, ended up by driving a 'bus in London; Holmes, Stephenson and Abell joined the constabulary; Richardson, Greenstock, Surrurier and McCanlis have been acting as dockers at Bristol, Hull and Liverpool.

'Isis' on Oxford cricket during the general strike, in *The Cricketer*, **1926**.

It is a matter of getting on with each other, doing things together, that's all I can say. It's civilised and it's cheerful, it's fun and a bit of competition just adds spice to it.

LORD SCARMAN, who conducted inquiry into the Brixton riots, at Brixton v Police cricket match, The Oval, **1981**.

The single most important change has been the decline of the personality player and the rise of the professional attitude . . . it is a product of the times, a tangent from Trade Unionism.

COLIN COWDREY, in *MCC*, **1976**.

Perhaps more than any other sport cricket is the white man's game. That is why they say when a man does anything that is not straightforward, 'That is not cricket'.

Advert in *The Cricketer*, **1924**.

No country which has cricket as one of its national games has yet gone Communist. On this I found my trust that the new regime in West Indian Grenada will turn out to be not so extreme Left-Wing as predicted.

WOODROW WYATT in the *Sunday Mirror*, **1979**.

The word 'England' suggests many different ideas to different kinds of Englishmen; the greater part of our juvenile population, for instance, think of it simply as that portion of the globe which, from time to time, produces 11 good cricketers to play Test matches (and sometimes to win them) against Australia or South Africa.

PRINCE OF WALES speaking at St George's Day Banquet, Guildhall, **1923**.

Cricket is certainly among the most powerful links which keep our Empire together. It is one of the greatest contributions which the British people have made to the cause of humanity.

RANJITSINHJI.

Cricket has done more to consolidate the Empire than any other influence.

LORD HARRIS, *A Few Short Runs*, **1921**.

On the cricket grounds of the Empire is fostered the spirit of never knowing when you are beaten, of playing for your side and not for yourself, and of never giving up a game as lost . . . the future of cricket and the Empire is so inseparably connected.

LORD HAWKE, in introduction to Warner's *Imperial Cricket*.

Sport an Aid to Empire Building.
Cricket and Football Leading Factors.

The Cricketer headline, **1927**, on an article by George Dewe pleading for more
cricket and rugby in Canada to attract British emigrants.

How often have I wished that all the political leaders in all the
countries of the Empire were cricketers! For if they had undergone
the training and the discipline of the great game, I am sure they
would find it easier than they appear to do at present to think
first and last of the team.

JAM SAHIB of Nawanagar, cricket dinner at Merchant Taylors' Hall, in honour of
touring Australians, **1930**.

When I first picked up a bat as a child, politics and sport were
simply two subjects at opposite ends of a newspaper.

BARRY RICHARDS.

Say that cricket has nothing to do with politics and you say that
cricket has nothing to do with life.

JOHN ARLOTT.

> Your fleet you've scuttled, and your War Lords fled,
> Your toasted day has turned to night instead,
> Crime upon crime, your last crime now we see,
> You've pinched the colours of I. Zingari.

LORD DARTMOUTH, Governor of I. Zingari, on Germany's adoption of red, black
and gold as its National colours after the First World War.

What a wonderful season it is going to be – strikes and German
arrogance permitting.

R. O. EDWARDS in *The Cricketer*, **1921**.

Did you see that, sir? That means war!

MCC member to colleague at Lord's when a green baize cloth was placed over
one of the Long Room busts, **1939**.

My successes with the Army are owing in a great measure to the manly sports of Great Britain, and one sport above all – Cricket.

Ascribed to a Duke of Wellington speech in the Lords by Arthur Haygarth (quoted by G. D. Martineau, *The Cricketer*, **1959**, who admits he has been unable to find the source).

'Co-operation in war' is one of the most important principles that a soldier has to learn. Let them learn this principle at cricket; it is just the same; it all boils down to 'team-work'.

'Cricket at Sandhurst', *The Cricketer*, **1921**.

Cricket, and for that matter all games, are part of the essential training of an officer.

As above.

Young ensigns and lieutenants, who had never seen a battle before, rushed to meet death as though they had been playing cricket.

DUKE OF WELLINGTON on the Battle of Waterloo.

The Battle of Britain was now in full swing, but we decided to carry on with the game as a number of boys had put their names down and I didn't want to disappoint them.

HENRY GRIERSON, founder and Honorary Secretary of The Forty Club, on their match v Public Schools at Richmond, August **1940**.

During the afternoon heavy aerial fighting developed between our fighters and the German bombers, and the sirens went. The boys were anxious to continue play, but there was just an outside chance of one being hit, so we sent them to the nearby shelters. I regret to record that the Forty Club repaired to the bar.

As above.

Carpets were laid on the pavé and the match took place, with occasional interruptions from shelling. During one of these breaks, cover point was hit by a piece of shrapnel, but, after first aid by the medical officer, who was also the umpire, the game went on.

BRIGADIER M. A. GREEN, on cricket in the Second World War in *Sporting Campaigner*, **1956**.

Field-Marshal Rommel . . . would have made a great cricket captain if his birthplace had been slightly different.

IAN PEEBLES.

If we had shown that kind of attitude and guts during the war that our cricketers have in the West Indies, Hitler would have walked over us.

BRIAN CLOSE, **1986**.

Say, when do they begin?

GROUCHO MARX, watching Middlesex bat at Lord's, **1960s**.

I don't think I can be expected to take seriously a game which takes less than three days to reach its conclusion.

TOM STOPPARD, playwright and cricket buff, on baseball in New York, **1984**.

If cricket is to continue as a spectacle to interest a public and provide them with entertainment, the great majority of players will have to show far more zest and attacking ability. Your committee is at one with the authority that declares there is nothing wrong with the game but only with the players' approach to it; unless this is remedied soon, most players will have lost the ability, through lack of practice, to play strokes, and the game will face an age of strokeless batsmen opposed by throwers and draggers – a complete prostitution of the art of cricket.

Warwickshire report, after attendances fell by more than half a million in a single year, **1959**.

I'm told that it was not until the first week of June 1946 that the
public was told that county cricket was dying, and of course the
game has been on its last legs ever since.

DOUG INSOLE, *Cricket From The Middle*, **1960**.

Cricketers do not expect anyone to watch three-day games.

PETER ROEBUCK, Somerset batsman, **1985**.

Without overseas players, the English county game would be
dead.

RICHARD HADLEE, *At The Double*, **1985**.

They should stop whining about overseas players. There are too
many old men in English cricket. Look at Ray Illingworth, at the
age of 50, Geoff Boycott and so many others like them – these
are the men who are stopping the young players coming through.

ASIF IQBAL on moves to reduce the number of overseas players, **1983**.

It would have been a paltry and unworthy thing to deprive
Australia, by means of a money bribe, of her finest batsman.

Wisden, on efforts to attract Victor Trumper, Australian, into English county
cricket, **1908**.

We regard it as Pantomime cricket.

CEDRIC RHOADES, Lancashire chairman, on England v Rest of the World series,
1970.

The public will no longer pay to stomach go-slow, draw-ridden
Test stuff.

CEDRIC RHOADES, Lancashire chairman, after poor crowds for England v India
series, **1971**.

There is a time in the year when Englishmen by common consent put the clock on an hour and by this simple expediency declare it to be summer. Of course you understand that doesn't change the English weather into summer weather. Nothing will. It is done because cricket is being regarded as a summer ritual game and so for its benefit summer has to be declared.

ANDRE DRUCKER, BBC Radio, **1954**.

I can hear you my lord, but where are you?

JOHN NEWMAN (Hampshire) joining his captain, Lionel Tennyson, at the wicket in bad light.

You can see the moon. How far do you want to see?

ARTHUR JEPSON, umpire, turning down appeal for bad light by Jack Bond in Gillette Cup tie, Lancashire v Gloucestershire at Old Trafford, **1971** (the match finished at 8.50 pm).

If I can see 'em, I can hit 'em.

DAVID HUGHES, before scoring 24 off one over to decide the above tie.

Throw down some sawdust, everybody put on top hats and red noses, and you've got the John Player League.

BRIAN CLOSE, **1969**.

For six days, thou shalt push up and down the line but on the seventh day thou shalt swipe.

DOUG PADGETT, Yorkshire batsman, offering 11th commandment, advent of Sunday League, **1969**.

You can give it everything in a one-day game, play at a pitch that would kill anyone who tried to keep it up six days a week all through the season.

Anonymous player to John Arlott on the Gillette Cup, **1963**, then in its first year.

You don't go on to bowl at half past eleven reminding yourself to save some energy for half past six; you know you can only bowl 15 overs and you give them all you've got . . . and even in the field you know you will be there less than four hours and you are on your toes and at full speed right through.

Same anonymous player to John Arlott.

In no case will Sunday play begin prior to 2 pm, so that those wishing to attend a Church Service and an afternoon's cricket may do both.

County committee report on advent of Sunday cricket, **1965**.

To a man of my age the introduction of the Sunday League has been nothing less than an act of cruelty.

TOM GRAVENEY, England and Worcestershire batsman, **1970**.

Professional cricketers are for the most part ultra-conservative in their approach to the game and I reluctantly predict that in one or two seasons the Sunday League games will become as stereotyped as the present county games.

'BOMBER' WELLS, Gloucestershire spinner, on advent of Sunday League, **1969**.

Limited-overs cricket is workshop cricket. It is the same as saying to golfers like Jack Nicklaus, Gary Player and Tony Jacklin, here is a wonderful and challenging course – you have got to be back in an hour and ten minutes. They would play no better than greenhorns. In real cricket, the player who has developed imagination and skill makes the game, but in the one-day match it is the other way round. The match dictates to the player.

BRIAN CLOSE, prior to his sacking by Yorkshire, **1970**.

There is a possibility that your ability as a player may well be analysed by future generations on your one-day statistics. That's the day I dread most.

ALLAN BORDER, Australian captain, **1985**.

I can hardly remember an innings I have played in one-day cricket.

GREG CHAPPELL, **1984**.

One-day cricket has killed outswing. Bowlers have got to come wide of the wicket and arrow the ball towards the leg side. They open up their bodies and become arm bowlers.

RICHARD HADLEE in *At The Double*, **1985**.

This game is injecting a dementia into the souls of those who play it.

BILL O'REILLY, *Sydney Morning Herald*, on effects of one-day cricket, **1982**.

It is surely the loveliest scene in England and the most disarming sound. From the ranks of the unseen dead for ever passing along our country lanes, the Englishman falls out for a moment to look over the gate of the cricket field and smile.

SIR JAMES BARRIE.

I doubt if there is any game in the world more animating or delightful than a cricket match – I do not mean a set match at Lord's ground for money, hard money, between certain gentlemen and players, as they are called – people who make a trade of that noble sport and degrade it into an affair of betting and hedgings and cheatings, it may be like boxing or horse racing . . . NO! The cricket I mean is a real, solid, old-fashioned match between neighbouring parishes where each attacks the other from honour and a supper, glory and half-a-crown a man.

MARY RUSSELL MITFORD, *A Country Cricket Match*. **1932**

We all started playing somewhere like this, and this is where we should all finish; back in village cricket that gave us our start.

EDDIE PAYNTER (Lancashire, England), then 58, on playing for Ingrow v Denholme.

Leave, O County Cricketer, leave for some fleeting moments, your perfect wicket, your 8 points, your struggle for first innings lead, your Bridge or Poker that goes on long after the rain has stopped, and the crowd has exhausted its patience and lost its shilling; come and watch us for nothing, and, if you have the heart to do it, come and laugh; if you have the soul, come and play.

R. C. ROBERTSON-GLASGOW, 'Village Cricket', *The Cricketer*, **1927**.

Has Tate bowled you with a fast off-break, third ball, before your eye was set? Come and be bowled first ball by Mr Muggridge, with a fast shooter, before you have taken guard. Then, indeed, you are a cricketer.

R. C. ROBERTSON-GLASGOW, as above.

Our lbw rule . . . is plain. One end you are out, even if struck on the head; the other end you are in, till you are bowled (undeniably) or caught (far from the ground). We admire this system, and are jealous of our traditions.

R. C. ROBERTSON-GLASGOW, as above.

But the football club was democratic, unlike the cricket club. I played cricket the first season, but resigned because the team seldom consisted of the best eleven men available; regular players would be dropped to make room for visiting gentry.

ROBERT GRAVES on village cricket at Islip, Oxfordshire, in the **1920s** (from *Goodbye to All That*, **1929**).

Villagers do not think village cricket is funny.

JOHN ARLOTT, foreword to Gerald Howat's *Village Cricket*, **1981**.

5

Philosophers All

Cricket Thoughts and Theories

What is human life but a game of cricket?

THE DUKE OF DORSET, **1777**.

There is no crisis in cricket, there is only the next ball.

W. G. GRACE.

They say onlookers see most of the game. But not always. The batsman at the other end sees more.

M. A. NOBLE.

What's the good of me going in? If I miss 'em I'm out and if I hit 'em I'm out. Let's start the next innings.

W. BUTTRESS (Cambridgeshire, 1860s), one of nature's No 11s, on being found up a tree when it was his turn to bat.

Look what the silly buggers have done now. Cost the club another 13s 6d.

JIM SMITH, taking the new ball to end a stubborn tenth wicket stand, Nottinghamshire v Middlesex, **1938**.

I haven't done it right often.

JIM LAKER, asked if his eight wickets for two runs for England against The Rest was his best bowling analysis, Park Avenue, **1950**.

A cricketer – a creature very nearly as stupid as a dog.

BERNARD LEVIN, *The Times* columnist, **1965**.

Nobody's perfect. You know what happened to the last man who was – they crucified him.

GEOFFREY BOYCOTT, answering criticism of his rate of scoring, **1979**.

If I knew I was going to die today I'd still want to hear the cricket scores.

J. H. HARDY.

I wanted to know who we were playing against.

WARWICK ARMSTRONG'S explanation for reading a newspaper in the outfield during the England v Australia test at the Oval, **1921**. England had used 31 players in the series.

Cricket is a situation game. When the situation is dead, the game is dead.

TREVOR BAILEY.

If we win the toss you will wish we had been a bit later still.

W. G. GRACE to a very angry Lord Harris when Grace's team arrived late at Canterbury because of a train hold-up, **1883**. Grace did win the toss.

I'm very sorry, my Lord, but I've been lunching with a lady.

C. J. M. FOX apologising to Lord Harris for a late return from lunch against Kent. Fox was batting at the time.

The game of cricket, philosophically considered, is a standing panegyric on the English character: none but an orderly and sensible race of people would so amuse themselves.

REV. JAMES PYCROFT, *The Cricket Field*, **1851**.

Pa, what is eternity for?
To see a cricket match played through.

Article in Boston newspaper, Lord Hawke's tour of United States, **1903**.

It has always puzzled me what the meaning of eternity is. Now I have a good idea.

PETER VAN DER BIJL, on the 'timeless' Test, South Africa v MCC in Durban, **1938/9** tour.

The public need to be educated up to cricket.

ROY KILNER, Yorkshire cricketer.

Comprehensives don't produce cricketers.

JIM LAKER.

To go to a cricket match for nothing but cricket is as though a man were to go into an inn for nothing but drink.

NEVILLE CARDUS, *Autobiography*, **1947**.

There's more ways of getting out than is shown in't rules.

WILFRED RHODES, **1930**.

The older I get, the better a cricketer I seem to become.

JIM LAKER, *Cricket Contrasts*, **1985**.

When 'it isn't cricket' has become an anachronism and a smear, cricket will be close to its deathbed.

J. M. KILBURN, *Yorkshire Post* cricket correspondent, in *The Cricketer*, **1971**.

It may not be cricket, but it's four.

E. M. GRACE pulling a ball from outside off-stump, which was considered unethical in the mid-nineteenth century.

Keep the left shoulder well forward and say your prayers.

A. N. HORNBY's precept for a cricketing life to the 9-year-old A. C. MacLaren.

In regard to the matter of praying, I expect those who do not use their left shoulder make up in prayer what they lack in shoulder work.

A. C. MACLAREN inveighing against the two-eyed stance, **1921**.

English cricket, for as long as I can remember, has been bedevilled by the cult of the left elbow.

LORD COBHAM, former MCC president, **1967**.

I'm taking that net you owe me from Durban, Mr Fender.

GEORGE BROWN, Hampshire and England batsman, explaining ultra-cautious innings to Percy Fender (who had refused to bowl at him on South African tour the previous winter); Hampshire v Surrey at Bournemouth, **1923**.

I realised just in time that unless I put bat to ball, I'd have to change in another dressing room.

GLENN TURNER, **1983**.

I think I know what that 'B' on your cap stands for.

JOHN DANIELL, Somerset captain, to opposing batsman who had spent four hours accumulating 50.

I play best when I'm surrounded by people who appreciate me.

GEOFFREY BOYCOTT, **1980**.

It's not comforting to feel I will no longer be a power in the land. I have found personal success very gratifying. I think it's going to be hard for me to drop out of it all.

JACK HOBBS, retiring from Test cricket, BBC radio, **1930**.

When I walk off a cricket ground for the last time – whenever that will be – it will be with an enormous sense of relief.

BARRY RICHARDS, 1978.

Who ever hoped like a cricketer?

R. C. ROBERTSON-GLASGOW, *Cricket Prints*, 1943.

I regularly wanted to lock myself in the toilet if I got out. I wanted to be alone.

GLENN TURNER, Worcestershire and New Zealand batsman, 1970.

You see the highlights. I see the failures. For motivation purposes, the failures are more important to me.

TIM ROBINSON, England batsman, 1985.

I couldn't help thinking that some of Kent's followers felt I was in the side because of my father. If I was out for nought, people would come up and say: 'How did you get a duck with your cricketing background?'

CHRIS COWDREY, about his Kent and England father, Colin, 1980.

People no longer ask me if he advises me because it's obvious he doesn't . . . or if he does, that I'm taking no notice!

CHRIS COWDREY, on comparisons with his father.

You lead in May, and I shall catch you in June.

PHILIP MEAD to Hampshire team-mates having pre-season nets.

I've just one ambition, I reckon. To have one innings early on in the Tests and see the buggers take a third new ball . . . that's what I want, and I'll bore them to death if need be.

GEOFFREY BOYCOTT, before England's West Indies tour, 1981.

There was no triumph in me as I watched the receding figure. I felt like a boy who had killed a dove.

ARTHUR MAILEY on bowling his idol Victor Trumper in a Grade match in Sydney (Redfern v Paddington).

I used to bowl tripe, then I wrote it, now I sell it.

Notice above Arthur Mailey's butcher's shop near Sydney.

My word, I know what all the problems are. I've failed at everything.

JOHN ARLOTT, asked whether playing first-class cricket would have been an advantage in his job, farewell broadcast, BBC Radio, 1980.

I can see I'm going to have to do a lot of bowling if I play for this side. I think I'd better cut my run down.

'BOMBER' WELLS, who bowled off three paces, after début for Gloucestershire at Bristol.

I can bowl so slow that if I don't like a ball I can run after it and bring it back.

J. M. BARRIE, 1926 (from Neville Cardus's *Autobiography*, 1947).

When you're an off-spinner there's not much point glaring at a batsman. If I glared at Viv Richards he'd just hit me even further.

DAVID ACFIELD, Essex, 1982.

Never mind, I've got a little kid at home who will make it up for me.

'POOR FRED' TATE, after dropping the catch that lost England the Old Trafford Test v Australia, 1902.

Ay, eight for thirteen; and if tha'd been half awake, it'd have been eight for 12.

EMMOTT ROBINSON replying to Alan Shackleton's congratulations after the latter had missed a half chance at cover point; Yorkshire v Cambridge University.

I was hoping they'd leave Malcolm Marshall on and not bring on John Southern.

PETER ROEBUCK, Somerset opening batsman, on his preference for pace rather than left-arm spin, Somerset v Hampshire **1983**, in *It Never Rains*.

If I ever bowl a maiden over, it's not my fault.

ARTHUR MAILEY, Australian spin bowler.

The dot ball has become the Holy Grail.

COLIN COWDREY, **1982**.

OCCUPATION: net bowler.

JACK BIRKENSHAW, Leicestershire all-rounder, filling in immigration cards during England's tour of India, **1972/3**.

There's no rule against bowling fast.

CLIVE LLOYD, West Indies captain, **1985**.

Wouldn't it be better if I got into the fridge?

QASIM OMAR, Pakistan batsman, receiving ice-pack treatment for bruising from Australian fast bowlers, Perth Test, **1983**.

I kept smiling at Thomson, hoping to keep him in a good mood.

RANJIT FERNANDO, 5ft 2in Sri Lankan batsman, as two of his team-mates were hospitalised by Jeff Thomson in a World Cup match, **1975**.

I'll have quite a rugged countenance by the time I'm finished.

MIKE BREARLEY, England captain, hit on the nose by Ghavri, Indian bowler, MCC v India at Lord's, **1980**.

Luckiest duck I ever made.

DON BRADMAN, after Aborigine Eddie Gilbert produced fastest spell he had ever faced, **1931**.

Dear, dear, now I shan't see Len bat.
Never mind, you can see me bat . . . if you don't run me out.

Exchange between DEREK MORGAN and LES JACKSON (Derbyshire) after Jackson
had dismissed Hutton quickly in one of Morgan's first appearances.

Thank God it wasn't twins!

Hampshire batsman, on learning Larwood's wife had given birth to a daughter.

I suppose I can gain some consolation from the fact that my name
will be permanently in the record books.

MALCOLM NASH, struck for six sixes in an over by Garfield Sobers, Glamorgan v
Nottinghamshire at Swansea, **1968**.

Go on Hedley, you have him in two minds. He doesn't know
whether to hit you for four or six.

ARTHUR WOOD, Yorkshire's wicket-keeper to Hedley Verity at Bramall Lane as
South African batsman H. B. Cameron took 30 off one over, **1935**.

You woke up in the night time and your arm was still going round.

L. O. 'B. FLEETWOOD-SMITH, left-arm wrist spinner, heavily punished during Len
Hutton's 364 v Australia at The Oval, **1938**. Hutton batted for 13 hrs 20 mins
(Fleetwood-Smith made his remarks on BBC Radio in 1970).

What is the good of an innings of 50 if that man drops a couple
of catches and lets by 40 or 50 runs? He has not only wiped his
own runs off the slate, but he has probably upset the bowlers into
the bargain.

A. E. R. GILLIGAN.

You don't expect to be beaten by a tail-ender – not at midnight
anyway.

ROGER KNIGHT, beaten Gloucestershire captain, after late night defeat in Gillette
Cup tie v Lancashire at Old Trafford, **1971**.

After all I've done for you, that's what you do to me!

W. G. GRACE, to Palmer, the Kent wicket-keeper, who stumped him minutes after the Doctor had given him stitches for a head wound caused by a bouncer.

You were simply caught in two-man's land.

KEN BARRINGTON to Brian Rose, England's tour of West Indies, **1980**.

It's not easy to bat with tears in your eyes.

DON BRADMAN, bowled second ball by Eric Hollies after ovation in his last Test at The Oval, England v Australia, **1948**.

If I find your spectacles, I'll send them on to your mother.

GEOFFREY BOYCOTT's quip to Paul Allott, England team-mate, when he was asked to field at long leg during a bomb alert, Old Trafford Test, **1981**.

They'll shoot you in the leg so that they can get you lbw again.

KEITH FLETCHER to slip colleague Tony Lewis, in Bombay after PLO murder threat, MCC tour of India, **1972/3**.

'Ere, Rupert, you've got to hit the ball to be lbw in this game. If you miss it, you can only be caught.

KEITH FLETCHER, Essex captain, to Somerset's Peter Roebuck, **1981**.

Out if I hadn't hit it, well bowled, out if I hadn't hit it.

W. G. GRACE after he had kicked away a ball which was about to bowl him and added insult to injury by running a single.

And I suppose if anyone's bowled it's just a nasty accident?

GEORGE GUNN, told umpires would be generous with lbws during a festival match, **1920s**.

Shall we put our heads down and make runs, or get out quickly and make history?

DON SHEPHERD joining Peter Walker with Glamorgan 11–8 v Leicestershire, **1971**.

We'll have to find it – I haven't any more.

GEOFFREY BOYCOTT to Dickie Bird during John Player League match at Huddersfield after Bird hàd managed to lose two of his contact lenses in a matter of seconds, **1980**.

I wouldn't say I have been ostracised by people since I became associated with World Series Cricket. There have been a few people who have been a little strange. In England they are too well bred to ostracise you openly.

RICHIE BENAUD, on WSC stigma, in *Howzat*, **1980**.

In England people do not speak to you unless they are firmly introduced with no hope of escape.

LEARIE CONSTANTINE, in *Cricket In The Sun*.

They say the fool of the family always goes into the church.

TED DEXTER, referring to a series of run-out disasters involving Rev. David Sheppard, Australia v England, **1963**.

Bad luck, Peter lad. The Reverend has more chance than most of us when he puts his hands together.

REV. DAVID SHEPPARD's version of Fred Trueman's celebrated one-liner. This time in dressing room, after dismissal of Peter Parfitt, Gentlemen v Players, **1962**.

If I say my prayers faithfully this is no guarantee that I shall make a hundred next time I go in to bat. I may make a duck. But I can make duck or hundred to the glory of God – by the way I accept success or failure.

REV. DAVID SHEPPARD, *Parson's Pitch*, **1964**.

You'll be no good with that stuff – you'll best get some ale down thee.

BRIAN JACKSON to Mike Hendrick in his early days in Derbyshire side.

No professional drunkard has ever made a great cricketer, nor
ever will.

'Quid', in *Jerks From Short Leg*, **1866**.

What, indeed, should I do at a dance with my dumpling of a
person tumbling about like a cricket ball on uneven ground?

MARY RUSSELL MITFORD, first women cricket writer.

I would rather go to a pub with half a dozen Northern
professionals than to all the studios, penthouses or Atheneums
and Saville Clubs in London.

NEVILLE CARDUS.

That's the end of cricket for me. I think I'll start running a
discotheque.

MUDASSAR after being given out lbw, Pakistan v England, **1978** (quoted in Wasim
Bari's diary).

I was too old for discos when I was 12.

BOB WILLIS, **1983**.

I don't try to be Joe Blow, the super-stud – it just happens.

JEFF THOMSON, from *Thommo*, **1981**.

Given the choice between Raquel Welch and a hundred at Lord's
I'd take the hundred every time.

GEOFFREY BOYCOTT, **1981**.

If only a quarter of the things written about me were true, I'd be
completely pickled by now and would have sired half the children
in the world.

IAN BOTHAM, beset by sex-and-drugs allegations, on England's tour of West
Indies, **1986**.

I have played my best cricket when I have been with my wife. If wives are accepted into the happy family, things will be very much better.

ALAN KNOTT, 1977.

Cricket is like sex films – they relieve frustration and tension.

LINDA LOVELACE, star of Deep Throat, visiting Lord's for England v India Test, 1974.

England's always expecting. No wonder they call her the Mother Country.

FRED TRUEMAN being asked for a final effort in a Test match.

I steer well clear of books on cricket, especially autobiographies, which I find rather boring. I'm in the game and I know all the politics, the manoeuvring and the petty jealousies that go on but hardly ever appear in a book.

GEOFFREY BOYCOTT, 1980.

A man who is engaged in heavy brainwork, such as writing a book about cricket . . . cannot be expected to be at his best on the cricket field.

RANJITSINHJI, in *The Jubilee Book of Cricket*, 1897.

You can count the number of books I have read on one hand. I don't even think you would fill the hand.

JEFF THOMSON, Australian paceman, 1975.

The season of 1896 was to me one of vast interest. It marked my first acquaintance with Plato and Fenners.

G. L. JESSOP.

It was Jung, I think, who said we learned from our failures, success merely confirming us in our mistakes. What can I learn from my failures at Test level?

MIKE BREARLEY, 1981.

I make no pretensions to oratory and I'd any day as soon make a duck as a speech.

W. G. GRACE, *Cricketing Reminiscences*, **1899**.

Mr Mayor and Gentlemen, I can't make a speech beyond saying thank-you but I'm ready to box any man in the room three rounds.

J. W. H. T. DOUGLAS, England cricketer and Olympic gold medallist at boxing, tour of Australia, **1911/12**.

I'd rather face Dennis Lillee with a stick of rhubarb than go through all that again.

IAN BOTHAM, cleared of assault at Grimsby Crown Court, **1981**.

After dinner I went to see Michael Redgrave in Daphne de Maurier's *Years Between*. I had had some 'years between' of my own, I reflected. I had ceased to be a cricketer and become an airman. Somehow, it is difficult to reverse the process. But, having ceased to be an airman, what should I do?

PAUL GIBB, Yorkshire amateur, from a disillusioned tour diary on MCC's tour to Australia, **1946/7**.

The only things that really keep me going are statistics.

RICHARD HADLEE, *At The Double*, **1985**.

My word, Herbert, if it hadn't been for my lumbago, we'd have brayed 'em.

PERCY HOMES (224) to Herbert Sutcliffe (313) after world-record partnership of 555 for first wicket v Essex at Leyton, **1932**.

People don't pay to watch me any more. They come to see me drop dead from exhaustion or old age.

BILL ALLEY, Somerset all-rounder, **1967**.

I have now resigned myself to the fact that I shall never achieve my ambition of scoring a hundred runs in a season.

PATRICK MOORE, astronomer and Sussex member, in *Wisden Cricket Monthly*, **1980**.

I'm going while you still ask why. I'm not waiting until you ask why not.

PATSY HENDREN, Middlesex and England batsman, on reason for his retirement.

Something just exploded in my head and I knew I had to get out or take the consequences. Three years of injuries have made me dread going out onto the field. If I had carried on I could have been a cripple at 35. My medical file is as thick as Wisden.

ALAN WARD, retiring from top-level cricket at 25, after being 'sent off' by Derbyshire's captain Brian Bolus, v Yorkshire at Chesterfield, 1973.

There comes a time when a man must realise that his cricket days are over. The thing first began to dawn on me when I noticed that the captain of the side, whenever he started to set his fielders, invariably began by saying, 'General, will you go point?'

BRIGADIER-GENERAL HUGH HEADLAM, in The Times, 1930.

He was gone at the knees, wore eye-glasses, was decidedly corpulent and showed distinct traces of his affection for good food and wine. I knew instinctively that this veteran must be the founder, financier and captain of his club, and that his side must lose more matches than it wins.

JACK HOBBS on meeting a 60-year-old cricketer.

I personally have a rooted objection to being called a 'veteran', a word which implies old age.

JACK HOBBS.

When he asked me if I could turn out, I thought he wanted me to play him at golf.

FRED TITMUS, after a 'phone call from Don Bennett, Middlesex's secretary, with a recall at age of 46, 1979.

Golf is a game to be played between cricket and death.

COLIN INGLEBY-MACKENZIE, ex-Hampshire captain.

I got bowled by a slow full toss, and I knew something was wrong with my eyes.

WILFRED RHODES, playing in Scotland a year after his retirement, **1931**.

Ah well, my feet aren't what they used to be.

HAROLD LARWOOD, awarded nought for plenty in a computer Test 'played' at Lord's between England and Australia, **1971**.

I'm off to another world, via the bat room.

AUBREY FAULKNER, of South Africa, in a suicide note he left before gassing himself, **1930**.

Well, the baby's dead and there's very little hope for the mother but I do believe I can pull the father through.

DR W. G. GRACE, interrupting a match to attend a difficult maternity case.

You'll be able to keep that unless we have another war.

PERCY FENDER to Steve O'Shaughnessy about the bat the Lancashire batsman used to equal Fender's world record century in 35 minutes, **1983**. (Fender's bat was destroyed in the Second World War.)

I bet the hall porter at the hotel is glad it's over. I had him making tea all night.

GEOFFREY BOYCOTT, after completing his 100th hundred in Headingley Test, against Australia, **1977**.

I see that Northamptonshire have a new bowler called Kettle. May I suggest to Keith Andrew that the best time to put him on would be ten minutes before the tea interval?

Letter in *The Cricketer*, **1959**.

Over the last few weeks I've felt that a fellow with his heart and feeling for the game was bound to break through.

SIR LEONARD HUTTON, when his son Richard won his first England cap, **1971**.

Cricket needs brightening up a bit. My solution is to let the players drink at the beginning of the game, not after. It always works in our picnic matches.

PAUL HOGAN, Australian comedian, **1983**.

I want to play cricket, it doesn't seem to mater whether you win or lose.

MEATLOAF, US rock singer, **1984**.

That's cricket, old sport.

FRANK BRUNO, following knockout victory against South African Gerrie Coetzee in a world heavyweight title eliminator in London, **1986**.

6
Close Encounters

Bodyline

I don't want to see you Mr Warner. There are two teams out there; one is trying to play cricket and the other is not.

BILL WOODFULL, Australian captain to Pelham Warner, the England manager, during Adelaide Test, **1932/3** series.

Bodyline was not an incident, it was not an accident, it was not a temporary aberration. It was the violence and ferocity of our age expressing itself in cricket. The time was the early thirties, the period in which the contemporary rejection of tradition, the contemporary disregard of means, the contemporary callousness, was taking shape.

C. L. R. JAMES, *Beyond A Boundary*, **1963**.

Bodyline bowling has assumed such proportions as to menace the best interests of the game, making protection of the body by the batsmen the main consideration. This is causing intensely bitter feeling between the players as well as injury. In our opinion it is unsportsmanlike. Unless stopped at once it is likely to upset the friendly relationships existing between Australia and England.

Text of cable from Australian Cricket Board to MCC, following Adelaide Test, **1933**.

We, Marylebone Cricket Club, deplore your cable. We deprecate your opinion that there has been unsportsmanlike play. We have fullest confidence in captain, team and managers and are convinced they would do nothing to infringe either the Laws of Cricket or the game. We have no evidence that our confidence has been misplaced. Much as we regret the accidents to Woodfull and Oldfield, we understand that in neither case was the bowler to blame. If the Australian Board of Control wish to propose a new Law or Rule, it shall receive our careful consideration in due course.

We hope the situation is now not as serious as your cable would seem to indicate, but if it is such as to jeopardise the good relations between England and Australian cricketers and you consider it desirable to cancel remainder of programme, we would consent, but with great reluctance.

MCC's cabled reply, **1933**.

> We have fought
> We have won
> And we have lost
> But we have never squealed before.

EARL OF DARTMOUTH, MCC elder statesman putting his feelings into rhyme after arrival of Australian telegram (quoted in *Cricket and Empire*, Sissons and Stoddart, **1984**).

Leg theory is generally a confession of impotence on the part of a bowler, and that should serve to cut it out of the game of any and every bowler claiming to be first class.

The Cricketer, **1925**.

If that little bugger can do that to him, what might I do?

HAROLD LARWOOD, watching Gubby Allen dismiss Don Bradman cheaply, England v Australia, **1930**.

Well, we shall win the Ashes – but we may lose a Dominion.

ROCKLEY WILSON, Winchester cricket coach, upon hearing that Jardine would captain MCC in Australia, **1932/3**.

Bowes should alter his tactics. He bowled with five men on the on-side, and sent down several very short-pitched balls which repeatedly bounced head high and more. This is not bowling, indeed it is not cricket, and if all the fast bowlers were to adopt his methods there would be trouble and plenty of it.

Editorial in *The Cricketer*, shortly before Bowes was drafted into England squad for the Bodyline series, **1932/3**.

If we don't beat you, we'll knock your bloody heads off.

England paceman BILL VOCE, to Australia's Vic Richardson, at the start of the Bodyline series, **1932/3**.

Well bowled, Harold!

D. R. JARDINE to Larwood as he hit Woodfull above the heart in Adelaide Test.

His excellency is a conscientious objector.

DOUGLAS JARDINE's remark when Nawab of Pataudi refused to join the legside field, the Bodyline series, **1932/3**.

If I happen to get hit out there Dad, keep Mum from jumping the fence and laying into those Pommy bowlers.

STAN MCCABE, resuming his innings of 187 in the Bodyline series, **1932/3**.

What about those fellows who marched to Kandahar with the fever on them?

DOUGLAS JARDINE's reply to Plum Warner, when informed that Eddie Paynter, Lancashire batsman, was in hospital and could miss the Test.

Do you think it is quite dignified that the greatest cricket match in the world between the two greatest cricketing powers should be interrupted by a certain amount of noise?

SIR PELHAM WARNER, requesting better crowd behaviour, Melbourne Town Hall.

No politics ever introduced in the British Empire ever caused me so much trouble as this damn bodyline bowling.

J. H. THOMAS, Secretary of State for The Dominions, during a luncheon speech at Claridges, **1933**.

I would rather lose the rubber than win over the bruised bodies of my opponents.

RANJITSINHJI, condemning bodyline tactics, **1933**.

Batsmen, particularly those who opened the innings for both countries since the First World War, had brought the trouble on themselves. In every dressing-room we heard the warning given by captains to opening batsmen: 'If you nibble at anything outside the off-stump, you'll get a good kick in the pants when you come back – even if you score a century.'

ARTHUR MAILEY on the background to bodyline.

Fast or fast medium bowlers in Australia are not offered many privileges or concessions as far as the atmospheric or ground conditions are concerned, and they found that sending down over after over pitched on or just outside the off-stump and seeing batsmen draw a disdainful bat away added to their frustration.

ARTHUR MAILEY.

Before that tour finished our boys were prepared to play shots a foot outside the off-stump, feeling perhaps that beggars can't be choosers.

ARTHUR MAILEY.

When everything is in favour of the batsmen (as in pitches abroad) I suppose it is natural that the captain and his bowlers should look for something extra or unusual in their methods of attack.

BILL BOWES on bodyline in *The Cricketer Spring Annual,* **1960**.

Leg-theory, even as bowled by Larwood, came as a natural evolution in the game. There was nothing sinister about it and nothing sinister was intended.

BILL BOWES, *Express Deliveries,* **1949**.

I'm sure my father wasn't a pisspot and a yobbo as portrayed.

JANE LARWOOD on the TV series 'Bodyline', **1985**.

Silly lies and bunkum.

HAROLD LARWOOD on 'Bodyline', **1985**.

Throwing

The straight-armed bowling, introduced by John Willes, Esq., was generally practised in this game, and proved a great obstacle against getting runs in comparison to what might have been got by straightforward bowling.

Morning Post report on 23 of Kent v 13 of England, **1807** (quoted in H. S. Altham and E. W. Swanton, *A History of Cricket*, 1926).

Willes threw down the ball in disgust, jumped on his horse, and rode away out of Lord's and out of cricket history.

Altham and Swanton on Willes being no-balled by Noah Mann, MCC v Kent, **1822** in *A History of Cricket* **1962**.

The elegant and scientific game of cricket will degenerate into a mere exhibition of rough, coarse, horse-play.

JOHN NYREN on the consequences of allowing round-arm bowling.

Far more latitude seems to be allowed to bowlers in England than in the Colonies, where unfair bowling is at once put down.

JOHN CONWAY, manager of the Australian touring team, **1878**, complaining about the prevalence of chuckers in Yorkshire.

I was twice bowled by Nash in Ephraim Lockwood's benefit match. Nash was just a real Lancashire 'chucker', slow left; but even if he had been fast no-one in those days seemed capable of even attempting to stop throwing. It was not until later that Lord Harris took a most worthy stand against this abuse, and thank goodness he did, or throwing might have been carried on to the present day.

LORD HAWKE, on his first pair in **1882**, in *Recollections and Reminiscences*, 1924.

Fast bowlers get massage in the back; Eddie got it in the crook of the arm.

SYD REDGRAVE of Queensland, on questionable action of his colleague Eddie Gilbert, Aborigine fast bowler, after his bouncers had hit three batsmen, **1935**.

Was I bowled or run out?

DOUG INSOLE, bowled by Tony Lock's quicker ball, The Rest v Surrey, The Oval, **1955**.

If allowed to get out of hand it (the throwing controversy) could lead to the greatest catastrophe in cricket history.

SIR DON BRADMAN.

If they stop throwing, cricket in Australia will die.

TOMMY ANDREWS, former Australian Test player, **1958/9** Test series.

Bowl him one for a change Burkie, you'll surprise him.

Colleague to Burke, New South Wales pace bowler, during throwing controversy in Australia; MCC tour, **1957/8**.

To bowl fast is a gift given to very few; traditionally only to those with either a vast body or a long flexible arm. Now we see thin men, unco-ordinated men, ordinary men, qualifying as fast bowlers.

ROBIN MARLAR on the effects of throwing, *The Cricketer*, **1960**.

One of the easiest ways of bowling a bouncer, if one's natural pace is below fast, is by throwing it. Loader's bouncer is everywhere regarded as the nastiest of all because it is so much faster than his normal ball and very accurately delivered.

ROBIN MARLAR, as above.

All over the world, I believe, there is a tie-up between throwing and bouncing. We must have a retaliatory bowler, think the selectors, and with lax administration of both the bumping and throwing laws a whole bevy of dubious bowlers capable of delivering the ultimate weapon, the bouncer, have arrived on the scene.

ROBIN MARLAR, *The Cricketer*, **1960**.

Yes, I'm the last of the straight-arm bowlers.

RAY LINDWALL replying to Bill Bowes's congratulations on his selection for Australia v England, **1958/9**.

We could never escape the wrangling, the arguing. It was all around us and we were part of it.

BRIAN STATHAM on the effect of the throwing controversy during the **1958/9** England tour of Australia.

One can readily appreciate Buller's predicament, and one cannot question his right to act as he did, but it was ironic that his action should be taken at a time when the players were engaged in a light-hearted knock about.

The Cricketer editorial, July, **1960**, on the no-balling of Griffin (S. Africa) for throwing in the knock-up game at Lord's after the Test's early finish.

It savoured of *opera bouffe* when, in a match of this character, Griffin was no-balled for not notifying the umpire that he was completing the over with under-arm deliveries.

As above.

No umpire enjoys calling bowlers for throwing. It is a very unpleasant task . . . but someone has to stop illegal bowling.

TOM SMITH, General Secretary of the Association of Cricket Umpires, in *The Cricketer*, July, **1960**.

Throwing is unfair. It is insidious, infectious and a menace to the game. It must be stopped and the exchange of cables between countries will not do it. Unless it is stopped before the Australians arrive, a serious position is imminent.

TOM SMITH, *The Cricketer*, July, **1960**.

The winning or losing of the Ashes is a small matter compared with the risk of 'the greatest catastrophe in cricket history'. Rather than that, I believe it would even be better for our Board of Control to declare a moratorium so far as games against the Australians were concerned.

E. W. SWANTON.

English umpires would be instructed not to call on the field for suspect delivery any Australian bowler on the 1961 tour prior to June 7 1961 . . .
From June 7 1961, umpires are instructed to implement Law 26 on the field in the normal way according to their judgement.

MCC statement, 3rd November **1960**.

The trial period can be considered only a retrograde step . . . It is to be regretted that 'insidiousness', 'unfairness', and 'action detrimental to the game' (terms that have been freely used) are to be allowed a free-for-all period.

TOM SMITH.

You must be the greatest thrower-out of all time, but I think your action is suspect.

KEN (SLASHER) MACKAY to Joe Soloman for the run-out which tied the Australia v West Indies Test match, **1960/61**.

If his action is the same as it was, he would be no-balled walking down the gangplank at Tilbury.

England player on Meckiff's illegal action, **1963**.

His (Meckiff's) selection represents one of the most fantastic somersaults in cricket policies in our time.

W. J. O'REILLY on the recall of Meckiff for the Australia v South Africa tests of 1963/4 after the throwing controversy.

His selection has surprised but delighted practically all followers of the game in this country.

LINDSEY HASSETT.

I think our selectors have insulted South Africa by this move. All Meckiff's team-mates, though once divided, now agree he infringes Law 26.

RAY LINDWALL.

I do not support the selection of men who do not play to the rules.

CLEM JONES, Lord Mayor of Brisbane and Queensland representative on the Australian Board of Control.

I bowled Meckiff for hundreds of overs before umpires who approved his delivery and I have accepted their decision. Now that an umpire does not accept Meckiff's delivery, I accept that decision too. I will not bowl him again.

RICHIE BENAUD, Australian captain, after Meckiff had been no-balled for throwing in the first test, Australia v South Africa at Brisbane **1963/4**.

I know that Richie did the right thing, because he is behind every player.

IAN MECKIFF on Benaud's decision to take him off after he was no-balled in his first over.

It defies description – the feeling that hits players when there is a no-ball called for throwing . . . One can only assume that the game was carried on by instinct for a while, for the Australian players were not . . . 'with it'.

RICHIE BENAUD after Meckiff had been called at Brisbane.

I'm afraid this is the end, Dad.

RICHIE BENAUD to Ian Meckiff after the latter had been no-balled for throwing,
Australia v South Africa **1961/2**.

If they re-write the Laws and say that double-jointed people must
not be allowed to play the first-class game, well, fair enough.

HAROLD RHODES, Derbyshire paceman, during throwing controversy, **1966**.

South Africa and Apartheid

There can be no normal sport in an abnormal society.

Stance of South African Cricket Board, who run non-white competitions.

All I know is there is a nice golf course there.

ALEC BEDSER, chairman of selectors, asked about intricacies of Gleneagles
Agreement at height of Robin Jackman Affair; Tour of West Indies, **1980/81**.

South Africa should never have had Test status. The South
African Cricket Association does not represent the whole country.
It is a fact that the Association practised rigid apartheid long
before the government required it and they show no desire to end
it.

DENNIS BRUTUS, Secretary of the non-white South African Sports Association,
1960.

If the game can conceivably be used as a force to unite conflicting
racial groups, there seems to be no reason why South African
cricket should not recover from its present malaise.

J. P. FELLOWS-SMITH after the disastrous **1960** tour of England was followed by
South Africa's withdrawal from the Commonwealth and consequent loss of
ICC membership.

All our sportsmen have proved they are willing to meet players from any land provided it does not conflict with the policies over which they have no say.

JACK CHEETHAM, former South Africa captain, on the ICC decision to defer question of his country's readmittance to the ICC after leaving the Commonwealth.

Some of those who said I should have kept my mouth shut held that a parson should only speak about religion . . . such men want to think of life as a series of watertight compartments. 'Don't let your home life affect your business life. Don't let your business life affect your sport. Don't let religion affect the way you run the other parts of your life.' But the whole point is that, if Christ is Lord, there are no other parts of life.

REV. DAVID SHEPPARD, on speaking out against cricketing links with South Africa, in *Parson's Pitch*, **1964**.

Teams comprising whites and non-whites from abroad cannot be allowed to enter.

JAN DE CLERK, South Africa's Minister of the Interior, in a written directive to sports organisations before the Basil D'Oliveira affair.

We will never know the whole truth concerning the omission of D'Oliveira from the MCC touring party to South Africa . . . I come down on the side of honesty, a good honest piece of bungling by good honest men.

TED DEXTER's verdict as Cape coloured Basil D'Oliveira was first omitted, and then chosen, for MCC's tour of South Africa, **1968**.

Thinking of you very much today. Love to you both. Penny Cowdrey.

Inscription on bouquet of flowers after D'Oliveira was not chosen; her husband, Colin, was captain.

Guests who have ulterior motives usually find they are not invited.

South African Prime Minister VORSTER, when hearing Basil D'Oliveira, overlooked in England's tour party, intended to cover series as a journalist, **1968**.

The generous treatment by the selectors of D'Oliveira this summer has been the cricket mystery of 1968. It has given the impression that they were anxious to put him into the touring side and so embarrass the South African authorities . . . the more chances he had, the more obviously he became a liability to the team.

E. M. WELLINGS, *Evening News*, **1968**.

It's not the MCC team. It's the team of the anti-apartheid movement. We are not prepared to have a team thrust upon us.

South Africa's Prime Minister VORSTER when D'Oliveira drafted into MCC tour party in place of injured Tom Cartwright, **1968**.

The selectors' brief throughout was simply to chose the best available team on cricket merit.

MCC statement on D'Oliveira affair, **1968**.

I wanted to be a cricketer who had been chosen as a cricketer and not as a symbol.

BASIL D'OLIVEIRA, in *The D'Oliveira Affair*, **1968**.

What has been done is tantamount to punching a wife for the crimes of her husband.

PETER POLLOCK, South African pace bowler, on the cancellation of their England tour, **1970**.

You do not cut yourself off from friends.

RAMAN SUBBA ROW, pressing for South Africa tour of England to go ahead, **1970**.

I'm ashamed I was so late in coming to the realization of the South African evil.

REV. DAVID SHEPPARD, Bishop Of Woolwich, **1970**.

This is a matter of principle. I like to judge people for what they are, not for what they look like.

PETER LEVER, asking to be released from Lancashire contract, for anticipated South Africa visit to Old Trafford, **1970**.

I abhor apartheid and this is to be my personal protest. Anything up to 100,000 locusts will be let loose at a particular ground and I think the plan is foolproof. They will ravage every blade of grass and green foliage. The greatest care will be taken to ensure they are in the correct physiological stage. So that their insatiable appetites will not be impaired they will not be fed for 24 hours before the moment of truth.

DAVID WILTON-GODBERFORD, biology student, planning to disrupt South African tour of England, **1970**.

We cricketers feel that the time has come for an expression of our views. We fully support the South African Cricket Association's application to include non-whites on the tour to Australia if good enough and, furthermore, subscribe to merit being the only criterion on the cricket field.

Statement by South African players at Newlands, in Transvaal v Rest of South Africa match, after walk-off in protest against the government's refusal to allow integrated cricket, **1971**.

My greatest wish is to see South Africa back in Test cricket.

FRED TRUEMAN, **1979**.

That list is of no importance.

ROBIN JACKMAN, on the United Nations blacklist of players who had visited South Africa, **1981**.

Every 'phone that I am talking to you on is listened to.

IAN BOTHAM, during deportation of Robin Jackman from Guyana for South African links. England's tour of West Indies, **1981**.

I intend to press on, because I know there are a lot of top cricketers from England, Australia and New Zealand who would love to play in South Africa. They resent being dictated to about where they can play cricket, and sponsors are lining up here to pay for a tour by an international side of Test class.

DAVID SMITH, South African businessman, **1981**.

I will accept your book – because you caused me so much trouble.

INDIRA GANDHI, Indian Prime Minister, when Geoffrey Boycott presented her with a copy of the book in which he condemns apartheid, Delhi, at start of England tour, **1981**.

Wouldn't you go to Russia or China if it was a free trip with all expenses paid?

GEOFFREY BOYCOTT, during England's tour of India, explaining that he would still visit South Africa, **1981**.

When I toured South Africa with Oxbridge Jazzhats, I became physically ill for a week. We were being used for propaganda. I will never return there.

DEREK PRINGLE, **1982**.

I've got nothing on my conscience. I'm just here to play cricket.

PETER WILLEY, on English 'rebel' tour to South Africa, **1982**.

Legally they're absolutely clean. And morally they're cleaner. What they've done is put an end to a lot of the hypocrisy which has existed in the cricket world for far too long.

MIKE PROCTER, **1982**.

These men have risked their careers. They have taken a stand against hypocrisy.

JOE PAMENSKY, President of South African Cricket Union, on England's 'rebel' tourists, **1982**.

They are selling themselves for blood-covered krugerrands.

GERALD KAUFMAN, Labour Party politician, **1982**.

Sporting boycotts have become the shopsoiled currency of international diplomacy . . . some sportsmen are not very adept at political complexities.

The *Guardian* editorial, **1982**.

They are being used as political pawns and have succumbed to greed.

KEN TURNER, Northants secretary, **1982**.

Being a Christian I cannot imagine a missionary saying: 'We won't go there until apartheid is finished.'

ALAN KNOTT, explaining why he joined South African 'rebel' tour, in *It's Knott Cricket*, **1985**.

Isn't he the one who is a traitor?

Small boy about Graham Gooch at Essex benefit match, in wake of South African 'rebel' tour, **1982**.

I was disgusted by the crowd's reaction. I came here to play cricket. Politics are nothing to do with me.

ALVIN KALLICHARRAN, West Indies batsman, after hostile reception from black section of Capetown crowd, **1982**.

How can you play cricket with a bloke and then not be allowed to sit in a railway carriage with him?

KEN MCEWAN, on ordering out of West Indian Colin Croft from a 'whites-only' section of South African train, **1983**.

We are accepted for what we are, professional cricketers. Not black or white or pink or purple. I doubt if I can convince people back home of what I've seen. People may have their set ideas. They may not want to hear what I tell them.

COLIN CROFT, **1983**.

Rod felt there were more things to life than playing cricket for his country.

DONNA MCCURDY, wife of Rod McCurdy, Australian pace bowler who joined 'rebel' South African tour, **1985**.

That man's got to appreciate it's a sensitive situation. He's a white man who has played in South Africa and he can't shout at a black man in the West Indies.

LOCKHART SEBASTIEN, of Windward Islands, after Greg Thomas challenged a batsman to 'walk', England tour, **1986**.

Gobbledegooch.

South African newspaper headline on Gooch's statement which overcame West Indian objections to his inclusion in the England tour party, **1986**.

The Packer Circus

Cricket is the easiest sport in the world to take over. Nobody bothered to pay the players what they were worth.

KERRY PACKER, **1977**.

The whole basis of this is an ideal – but nobody is going to do it for peanuts.

TONY GREIG, England captain revealing plans for Packer series, **1977**.

The plight of the modern cricketer is certainly not the best. Many who've been playing eight years or more are living on the bread-line. In the winter they go abroad coaching, leaving their families behind. Test cricketers are also not paid what they're worth. As a result of this action, cricket may in five or ten years' come into line with· tennis and golf. Then, if a young man is faced with a decision which to play, he can choose cricket with confidence. People who give up their lives to a game should be rewarded accordingly.

TONY GREIG, at same Hove press conference, **1977**.

It makes me laugh when I hear the anti-Packer lobby telling me how to spend my winters. When I was a teenager, the same sort of people did not give a damn what I did between September and April.

GORDON GREENIDGE, **1980**.

The administrators have had 100 years to improve pay and conditions for the players and they haven't made any progress.

MUSHTAQ MOHAMMED, in Peter McFarline's *A Game Divided*, **1977**.

I have no desire to be a hack bowler up the bush with Packer.

RODNEY HOGG, Australian quickie, **1978**.

An example of the Lord's guidance came for me with my decision to join Packer's World Series Cricket.

ALAN KNOTT, *It's Knott Cricket*, **1985**.

It was always 'Kerry says this' and 'Kerry says that', like a speak-your-weight machine.

BOB TAYLOR on Packer players, in *Standing Up, Standing Back*, **1985**.

In affectionate remembrance of International Cricket, which died at Hove, 9th May, 1977. Deeply lamented by a large circle of friends and acquaintances. R.I.P. NB – The body will be cremated and the Ashes taken to Australia and scattered around the studio of TCN9 in Sydney – NTJCBM.

Notice placed by three Australian journalists in *The Times*, **1977**.

I have always said that any man worth his salt will, if picked, play for England whether at home or abroad.

TONY GREIG, **1976**.

His action has inevitably impaired the trust which existed between the cricket authorities and the captain of the England side.

TCCB cricket council, sacking Tony Greig as England's captain after announcement of Packer Circus, **1977**.

When I went into this I knew I was putting my captaincy on the line and I think that was very unselfish of me.

TONY GREIG, accused of selling-out by joining Packer, **1977**.

There is a little bit of the whore in all of us, gentlemen, don't you think?

KERRY PACKER, meeting Australian Board of Control to discuss TV rights, **1976**.

From now on, it is every man for himself and let the devil take the hindmost.

KERRY PACKER, leaving ICC meeting at Lord's, **1977**.

I've read a lot about Genghis Khan. He wasn't very lovable. But he was bloody efficient.

KERRY PACKER, **1977**.

It's unfortunate we Australians inherited the English mentality rather than the American.

KERRY PACKER, the *Guardian*, **1977**.

You British reckon everything can be solved by compromise and diplomacy. We Australians fight to the very last ditch.

KERRY PACKER, **1978**.

They are dedicated lovers of the game who nevertheless found it hard fully to understand the feelings and aspirations of those who seek to make their livings out of it.

MR JUSTICE SLADE, about the cricketing establishment, during High Court ruling that ban on Packer players was illegal, **1977**.

I've heard the only way to get out of a Packer contract is to become pregnant.

RAY STEELE, treasurer of Australian Cricket Board, during High Court hearing on Packer Affair, **1977**.

Tests are not built in a day.

MUTTHIAN CHIDAMBARAN (India), High Court.

They want the penny and the bun.

GEOFFREY BOYCOTT, High Court.

When a Yorkshireman shakes your hand that's all you need.

GEOFFREY BOYCOTT, High Court.

Wars are not won by appeasement.

W. H. WEBSTER, chairman of ICC, High Court.

Yesterday in the Australian Cricket Board's match in Brisbane, the Australian and Indian batsmen managed only 17 fours between them in a day's cricket. And in the WSC Super Test Australian and West Indian batsmen knocked out a massive 87 fours and three sixes. This alone is enough to stamp WSC's first Super Test as memorable and far superior to what went on in Brisbane, superior for cricketers, superior for crowds and superior for television. And that is how it will always be as long as the best are playing the best.

WSC press officer CHRIS FORSYTH, release during first World Series match, **1977**.

It is perhaps just as well that Mr E. W. Swanton, a cricket writer of much distinction, is now retired and living in Kent.

IAN WOOLDRIDGE, *Daily Mail*, on first floodlit match in Packer circus, Melbourne, **1977**.

Can't see Wayne Daniel, never mind the ball.

Packer World XI batsman on floodlit cricket, **1977**.

Wake up, you lazy lot! You've got to get used to this daytime cricket!

MUSHTAQ MOHAMMED to World XI colleagues on bus taking them to a rare morning start in Packer's World Series, **1978**.

I do not know that Test cricket can be saved. I hope so but I am not convinced. People will no longer sit through five days of a match. Those days are long gone. People don't go to watch beautiful defensive shots or the battle of tactics any more. Unless something is done to change the rules and the manner in which it is played, then officials will have a hard time to make it attractive.

LYNTON TAYLOR, Channel 9 executive, **1978**.

There is no doubt the centre of cricket has moved out of England and is now in Australia.

LYNTON TAYLOR, Channel 9 executive, **1985**.

7

Lords and Masters

MCC, Selectors, Committees and Others

Disraeli once stated that a country lives by its institutions. This is certainly true of Great Britain; it is full of institutions. Some, like the Royal National Lifeboat Association, are the envy of the world; others, like the House of Lords, are the target of venegary (sic) politicians and music-hall comedians. Midway between the two, more sedate than the former and less democratic than the latter, lies the MCC.

LORD COBHAM, MCC Treasurer, **1964**.

It is perhaps seldom appreciated to what lengths the Committee of the MCC is prepared to go to achieve a right decision on some point of cricket lore.

LORD COBHAM.

A discussion was held on the implication of the measurements to be used following the introduction of the metric system. The pitch (22 yards) will be 20.117 metres. The Dutch and Danish delegates stated that no difficulties need be anticipated with regard to the circumference of the ball.

ICC minutes, **1969**.

Cricket is a stalwart Goliath striding across the British Empire. MCC is his devoted wife, anxious only to further his best interests. Cricket and MCC will never be divorced. Therefore, they are a very old-fashioned couple but will go on happily united as long as the game is played.

SIR HOME GORDON, to Cross Arrows dinner, Lord's, **1929**.

No human institution is perfect, but it would, in my humble opinion, be impossible to find nicer men than those who constitute the government of Lord's.

SIR PELHAM WARNER, *Lord's 1787–1945*, **1946**.

I have been a member of the committee of the MCC and of the Conservative Cabinet and by comparison with the cricketers the Tories seemed like a bunch of Commies.

LORD MONCKTON at the MCC special meeting on South Africa, **1968**.

(Lord Harris GCSI, GCIE, CB) is essentially the 'Big Man' at Lord's, and what MCC would do without him I do not know.

PELHAM WARNER, *The Cricketer*, **1921**.

At home and abroad in politics and sport, Britain will do better without the Tories and their friends of the Marylebone Cricket Club. Twenty years ago *Tribune* first made the demand that the MCC should be nationalised. Now everyone can see the wisdom of our policy.

MICHAEL FOOT, in *Tribune*, after poor start to MCC's tour of Australia, **1958/9**.

I had barely eaten my first meal on earth before my father wrote off to friends in England asking them to put my name down for MCC membership.

COLIN COWDREY, *MCC*, **1976**.

It seems there is one rule for Botham and one rule for the rest.

Yorkshire committee member after Botham had been reprimanded for dissent and Bairstow given a suspended ban for the same offence, **1985**.

The Establishment seem to want my ability but not me.

GEOFFREY BOYCOTT, *In The Fast Lane*, **1981**.

You've got to get on with the powers that be, to tug the forelock.

PHIL EDMONDS, **1983**.

The visit to the dressing-room of a senior committee-man, watch-chain dangling, smacked of a Dickensian mill-owner's visit to a shop-floor. The players would stiffen into attitudes of modest respect. And if the committee man's mien had a benevolent aspect, that was probably because he stood to lose nothing by the workmen's inefficiency.

MIKE BREARLEY on the Middlesex committee of the 1960s. *The Art of Captaincy*, **1985**.

Many of your committee members are sitting there for no better reason than it is good for their business or social image to do so. They are status seekers who would as quickly get themselves on the tiddleywinks committee if that game should suddenly acquire prestige.

'BOMBER' WELLS, Gloucestershire spin bowler, **1970**.

They were more interested in the social pecking order than the future of the club. All they did was sit on the sidelines and criticise everything we did.

GEORGE HUGHES, businessman, about Derbyshire committee, after resigning as chairman after only nine months, **1977**.

I maintain I can contribute more in one telephone discussion with the chairman, Ossie Wheatley, than all the amateurs in a hundred meetings on the subject of cricket.

TONY LEWIS, sacked from Glamorgan's cricket committee for non-attendance, **1980**.

I have the greatest affection for the county of my birth, but for the committee as a body, the greatest contempt.

W. G. GRACE, resigning as Gloucestershire captain, **1899**.

I thought things were changing with people like Gatting and Botham leading their counties. But Hampshire obviously still prefer public schoolboys. Perhaps I don't have enough initials – it's a handicap having only two.

TREVOR JESTY, leaving Hampshire for Surrey after being passed over for captaincy, **1985**.

You do have a private income, don't you?

Middlesex committee man to Mike Brearley on his appointment as captain.

Kent has got cricket badly and always has had. A sort of 1914–18 camaraderie exists between the gentry and the rest. Both are happy that the other knows its place.

ANGUS MCGILL, *Cricket Bag*, **1965**.

Hello Ken, I've been meaning to have a word with you. How's the wife and family? All right I hope. Oh, by the way, you're not being re-engaged for next season.

EDDIE HARRISON, chairman of Sussex's cricket committee, informing Ken Suttle in the Hove car park that he was not receiving a new contract, **1970** (quoted in John Snow's *Cricket Rebel*, 1976).

As we took our seats, he looked across at Tony Greig and said: 'Ah, you must be Greig because you're so tall.' Then he turned to me and said: 'I recognize you because I've seen your picture in the newspapers,' and finally he came to Ken Suttle and said: 'That means you must be Ken Suttle because the three of you were coming.'

JOHN SNOW on a Sussex committee man meeting the three at a winter cricket dinner after Suttle had completed a run of 423 consecutive appearances for the county.

Sussex have always been regarded as the amateur gin-and-tonic men of English cricket – well, I'm going to change all that.

TONY GREIG, Sussex captain, **1974**.

He's waiting for a benefit but he's not getting one. He wants more money but we're not giving it to him.

Kent committee man on an unidentified player.

The Chairman of the cricket committee would come into the dressing-room just before we were going out to play an important Gillette Cup match and start telling us how the Sussex Martlets had got on on Sunday. And he expected us to be interested.

JOHN SNOW.

The captains and committees of the sixties will have a lot to answer for in the course of time. They are making a drudgery of a beautiful game.

JOHN WOODCOCK, *The Times*, **1966**.

I would rather the Australians won 2–1 or 3–1 than go through the dismal business of four more draws.

DAVID CLARK, MCC manager in Australia, after first two Tests were drawn, **1970/71** tour. The captain, Illingworth, did not agree.

It's unbelievable, but it's the old bowler hat and the umbrella and the 'Morning Illingworth' – they're still back in the thirties, they really are.

RAY ILLINGWORTH, then at Leicestershire, on Yorkshire committee, **1973**.

When I left Yorkshire I received a letter from the secretary saying they were not going to offer me a contract which began: 'Dear Ray Illingworth', but the 'Ray' had been crossed out. They couldn't even bring themselves to call me by my first name or use a fresh piece of paper.

RAY ILLINGWORTH.

He should be able to put on a straw hat and walk around the ground to be greeted with a friendly 'Hello'.

REG KIRK, resigning as Yorkshire's chairman with one piece of advice for his successor, **1986**.

We don't make certain that a doctor is present and we don't intend to. Several doctors are keen followers of cricket and there are usually some present. There are always cars to take anyone to hospital if necessary.

MAJOR DOUGLAS CARR, of Derbyshire, in wake of kiss-of-life needed by Glamorgan's Roger Davis when struck in close-fielding position, Glamorgan v Warwickshire at Cardiff, **1971**.

His language was that of a navvy to a workmate, labouring on a building site, but his attitude was that of the CO to the humblest private.

JOHN HAMPSHIRE, *Family Argument*, **1983**, on Brian Sellers, Yorkshire cricket committee chairman and former captain.

If any spectator is prepared to ask for his money back, I am prepared to consider his application.

WILF WOOLLER, Glamorgan secretary, making Swansea loudspeaker announcement as Brian Close delayed Somerset's declaration, **1972**.

I don't care if it costs me my job. I was so upset I could have thrown my bowl of soup in his face.

ARTHUR FAGG, umpire, angered by Wilf Wooller's criticism over a delayed start the following day. Fagg told Lord's he would not stand again at Glamorgan while Wooller remained secretary, **1972**.

There were competent judges of the game then on the various committees in place of the Lord Mayors and other excellent business heads today, who lack, however, the one thing necessary to qualify thoroughly for the post – an inside knowledge of the game.

A. C. MACLAREN defending the **1880s/90s** method of the host county committee selecting the Test team.

The selection committee are not in the least likely to be influenced in their choice of a captain by the opinions of writers, expert or otherwise.

The Cricketer, 'Answers to Correspondents', 14th May **1921**.

Right: 'I heard one Yorkshireman mutter, none too affectionately, "Here comes t'clown," as the blond-dyed hulk stepped out of his car wearing black leather trousers and a deckchair blazer. Later that day . . . he paraded his thigh-length cowboy boots before me. Between the two fashion shows he struck a magnificent 60.' Mike Brearley on Botham at the 1985 Headingley Test

Below: 'Difficult to be more laid back without being actually comatose.' Frances Edmonds on David Gower

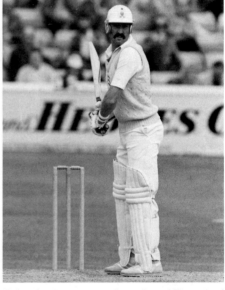

'A perfect running specimen, but I don't go to a Test to see running; if I wished to see that I would go to Crystal Palace to see Coe and Ovett.' Jack Fingleton on Michael Holding

'It has become my trademark and I'm proud of it because it was never introduced to my game as any sort of gimmick but an essential measure which has produced the desired results.' Graham Gooch on his controversial upright stance

Above: 'It was Jung, I think, who said we learned from our failures, success merely confirming us in our mistakes. What can I learn from my failures at Test level?' Mike Brearley

Above left: 'If the West Indies are on top, they're magnificent. If they are down, they grovel . . . I intend to make them grovel.' Tony Greig before the 1976 series which the West Indies won 3–0. Tony Greig with microphone, Clive Lloyd with trophy

Left: 'County bowlers are nothing if not philosophical. I'll be there in midsummer, running up to Sir Geoffrey — convincing myself he's going to pad up to a straight one.' Brian Brain

Right: 'It may surprise some people, but he actually likes cricket.' Kerry Packer demonstrating Mr Justice Slade's comments, 1977

Right: 'Blimey, the bugger can't bend as well can he?' Brian Close on Joel Garner

Below: 'I don't know why they bother to put the stumps out. None of those buggers are trying to hit them.' Graeme Fowler after a torrid two hours v. West Indies in 1984

'If we'd found out Dennis was the instigator, we'd have rubbed him out.' Greg Chappell on the Dennis Lillee–Javed Miandad altercation during the Australia v. Pakistan Test match, Perth, 1981

The Selection Committee . . . are open to receive opinions from those qualified to form them, and are delighted to consider them. The final selection of the captain, of course, rests entirely with them.

The Cricketer, 'Notes and Comments', 21st May **1921**.

Mr Bloody Warner will go to bed when I've finished with him.

CHARLIE PARKER, Gloucestershire's left-arm spin bowler, after a public scuffle with Sir Pelham Warner, whom he partly blamed for his lack of Test caps, **1929**.

I've always thought the selectors were a bunch of idiots. All they've done now is confirm it.

JEFF THOMSON, omitted from Australian tour party to England, **1981**.

'My God, look what they've sent me.'

A. C. MACLAREN on the team selected for England v Australia 4th Test, Old Trafford, **1902**. The selectors had left out Fry, Jessop and Barnes.

It was in the selection room that the rubber was lost that year.

G. L. JESSOP on his and Hirst's omission from the England team, Manchester, **1902**.

The selectors wanted to see Tate bowl on a wet wicket, and so they should.

A. C. MACLAREN's explanation for leaving out Hirst who was in the twelve in that match. MacLaren and Lord Hawke, the chairman of the selectors, had been sparring throughout the season.

The North is under no grievance and the sooner any imaginary sense of injustice is dispelled the better, because there is not the smallest justification for it.

LORD HAWKE, Yorkshire president, denying accusations of selection bias in favour of South of England, **1924**.

I think they must be mad.

PHIL EDMONDS on being omitted by Middlesex so they could play four seamers at Leicester, two days after he had helped England win the Ashes.

What benefit is there to anyone, Middlesex or me, to stay here in that capacity?

PHIL EDMONDS leaving Leicester after being made 12th man by Middlesex.

Who was that man I've been talking to?

England selector to Bob Willis. It was Phil Edmonds.

Good morning Roy, good morning Peter.

ALEC BEDSER, chairman of England selectors, greeting Ray East and John Lever in lift during Test trial, **1973**.

PBH instead of GBH.

JOHN WARR, at cricket dinner, describing arrival of P. B. H. May as chairman of England selectors, **1981**.

Gin-soaked old dodderers.

IAN BOTHAM on the England Selectors, **1986**.

8
Those Hallowed Turfs

Grounds

Lord's

Sir – Now I know that this country is finished. On Saturday, with Australia playing, I asked a London cabby to take me to Lord's and had to show him the way.

Letter to *The Times*.

After all, Lord's is Lord's.

Lord's attendant, requesting men to replace their shirts after complaints from women members. Middlesex v Yorkshire, **1959**.

Commodious grandstands engirdle the green oval, and in them, as if packed into pews, is Old England; squires in top hats; portly old gentlemen so empurpled by port wine and rare beef that their faces resemble thick round steaks left hanging in a butcher's shop; great ladies who haven't changed fashion since the dear Queen was on the Throne, and whose hats in consequence top them like huge crows' nests in dead trees; a firmament of parsons with parsonical umbrellas tightly in hand; Deans and Bishops in long black gaiters, cutaway coats and curly, black top hats quaintly hung with cords like wireless aerials.

New York World on the Oxford v Cambridge Centenary match, Lords **1927**.

Here verily is Old England, the silk hats a trifle shabby occasionally, perhaps, for taxes are high and incomes diminishing, but Old England, nevertheless, against a background of tallyho coaches and servile servants.

New York World.

Sir – I noticed one of the umpires today disgraced Lord's Ground by appearing with bicycle clips round his trousers during his work, surely rather infra-dig for the World's premier cricket ground.

Letter to the Secretary, MCC, posted up in Lord's pavilion, **1923**.

The clips did not affect his decisions, which were excellent.

The Cricketer comment.

Apart from the possible damage to the turf, Lord's seems to me to be hardly the place for impromptu 'soccer'.

Letter to *The Cricketer*, **1923**, about schoolboy games on the hallowed turf during the intervals.

Those in control at Lord's should remember that but for such men as these the historic enclosure might now be a German beer garden.

The Cricketer editorial on the refusal of admission to disabled soldiers because their chairs took up too much space, England v Australia, **1921**.

Australians will always fight for those 22 yards. Lord's and its traditions belong to Australia just as much as to England.

JOHN CURTIN, Australian Prime Minister, towards end of Second World War, **1945**.

Expect every ball to shoot and you will be in time if she rises; if watching too eagerly for the rise you will be too late if she shoots.

Advice to batsmen playing at Lord's in the **1820s/30s**.

The only respect in which its pitch resembled a billiard table was
the pockets.

H. S. ALTHAM on the same period.

My immediate reaction was. 'How on earth can major cricket be
played on this?'

JIM FAIRBROTHER, Lord's groundsman, on his first sight of the slope, in *Testing
The Wicket*, **1985**.

I shudder at the cold gloomy picture of Lord's or Melbourne 'Bull
Ring' after play is ended. The man who wrote 'The song is ended
but the melody lingers on' never, I'll warrant, played cricket on
either of these grounds.

ARTHUR MAILEY.

It has a fragrant atmosphere of past glories which acts as padding,
so to speak, to the more brittle surface that one is conscious of
at Sydney or Melbourne. The ghosts of the giants of other days
stalk in the shadows of every Test match ground, but they always
seem to be less ethereal or abstract at Lord's.

ARTHUR MAILEY.

I have heard radio and TV commentators mention 'a ball . . .
skidding through down the hill' and also 'bring one back up the
slope'. Now in the *Sunday Times* we read . . . of the ridge, not
to be confused with Vimy, that lies at the Nursery End. What
other hazards are there at the Mecca of cricket? Could you please
print a map of Lord's showing contours and any other unusual
features.

Letter to *The Cricketer*, **1960**.

Ebbw Vale

When I tap the pitch with my bat, someone else taps back.

PETER WALKER, of Glamorgan, on Ebbw Vale wicket, **1967**.

Hambledon

How those brawn-faced fellows of farmers would drink to our success! And then what stuff they had to drink! Punch! Not your new Ponche a la Romaine or Ponche a la Groseille, or your modern cat-lap milk punch – punch – punch be-deviled. But good, unsophisticated John Bull stuff – stark! – that would stand on end – punch that would make a cat speak!

JOHN NYREN, recalling cricket at Hambledon in the **1780s**.

I really wanted to see Hambledon, and had built up a romantic picture of what it should be like. We got there one afternoon, and searched the village for the ground. Eventually I found it . . . No charming village green, no church, just rather a bleak stretch of ground opposite the old pub. It was one of my great disappointments.

BOB TAYLOR, **1982**.

Headingley

There's a bastard in my family and it's sitting out there.

KEITH BOYCE, Headingley groundsman, on his Test wicket, **1985**.

Was it cosmic tragedy when somebody dug up the Test pitch with a knife and fork? Why couldn't they have moved the thing a yard or two? Elaborate explanations in *The Times* about the arcane conventions of this dotty game in no way persuade me that a just-possibly unjust prison sentence of twenty years isn't more important.

JAMES CAMERON, the *Guardian*, **1975**.

I'd throw them off the top of the pavilion. Mind, I'm a fair man, I'd give them a 50–50 chance. I'd have Keith Fletcher underneath trying to catch them.

FRED TRUEMAN, on the saboteurs of the Test wicket, **1975**.

Kent grounds

One sees more pretty cricket in Kent in a three-day match than can be seen anywhere else in England in a fortnight.

LEARIE CONSTANTINE, *Cricket In The Sun*.

Chatham

A small ground with limited stand and motor car accommodation. The wicket is probably the best wearing in the country, but the ground lacks the atmosphere of the other beautiful grounds that are allotted the Weeks. Ordinary admission is charged, and there is no band and very few tents.

The Cricketer, 'Notes and Comments', **1927**.

Mote Park, Maidstone

. . . with its 'tall, ancestral trees' (it) is captivating, but cricketers have no more appreciation of foliage than the foxhunters of violets in bloom.

J. A. H. CATTON in *Bat and Ball* (Ed. Thomas Moult). **1935**

St Lawrence, Canterbury

The social side of Kent cricket possesses some of the carnival spirit of the Continent, for each town is gay with bunting, illuminations, and entertainment. Nevertheless St Lawrence has the atmosphere of old times and the countryside. Marquees and tents, decorated and bright with flowers, are near the boundaries, with trees towering behind them.

J. A. H. CATTON.

Melbourne

After two overs at Melbourne there are practically no outside stitches, no glossy appearance, on the ball.

MAURICE TATE.

Old Trafford

There was a time when the weather was not responsible for some very awkward wickets at Old Trafford, at a time too when Walter Brearley was our fast bowler, which made some of our opponents wonder once or twice if our wickets were kept rough on purpose.

A. C. MACLAREN.

When my innings had not lasted more than twenty minutes, I managed in that short time to collect a full pocket of pebbles, which I bounced on the Committee room table on my way up to the dressing-room, informing our members of the true reason for our low scores.

A. C. MACLAREN on the Lancashire Committee's criticism of the team's low scores in the **1880s**.

I suppose if you don't play in gloom up here you never play at all.

ALAN KNOTT, **1981**.

The pit of hate.

HOWARD BOOTH, *Daily Mirror*, describing members' enclosure.

Oxford

The sole advantage of Port Meadow as a cricket pitch was the absence of boundaries. The chief disadvantage was that the city burgesses used the Meadow for the pasturage of their cows – graminvorous animals of casual habits.

KENNETH GRAHAME on cricket at St Edwards College, Oxford.

> Adown thy glades, all sacrificed to cricket,
> The hollow-sounding bat now guards the wicket
> . . .
> But the broad Parks, the city's joy and Pride,
> When once destroyed can never be supplied.

DR DODGSON (LEWIS CARROLL) in *The Deserted Parks*, opposing the proposal to permit cricket in the Parks, **1867**.

Scarborough

Someone asked me if it was true that I had hit a ball into Trafalgar Square and was it hit from Lord's or The Oval. When I said it was Trafalgar Square, Scarborough . . . he wasn't so much impressed.

C. I. 'BUNS' THORNTON on his six off A. G. Steel, **1887**.

Whatever Festival cricket may have been in the days of its inception, when luncheon intervals frequently varied according to the susceptible comfort of the players, it is a vastly different thing today. Though punctuality may interfere with port, such Elysiums as Scarborough and Hastings were certainly in my time as strictly conscious of the spectators' welfare as of the players'.

G. L. JESSOP.

I'd like to build a row of houses right across this wicket. Any more tricks like this and I'll be finished in 12 months.

FRED TRUEMAN after Warwickshire had scored 269 v Yorkshire, **1963**.

Sheffield

Fred Trueman's forever moaning about this wicket; but it's only an 'abit. 'E knows Wilfred's taken five wickets on 'ere and scored sixty odd, same day.

TOM PARKIN, groundsman at Bramall Lane.

Swansea

From the top of the hill top pavilion,
The sea is a cheat to the eye,
Where it secretly seeps into coastline,
Or fades in the yellow-grey sky;
But the crease marks are sharp on the green,
As the axe's first taste of the tree,
And keen is the Welshman's assault,
As the freshening fret from the sea.

JOHN ARLOTT, opening lines of *Cricket At Swansea*.

Sydney

The Hill at Sydney used to be amusing, sharp and cutting, but not unfriendly; now it's simply foul-mouthed and crude.

GEOFFREY BOYCOTT, **1979**.

I enjoyed it, but if I go back again I'll wear a tin hat.

LAURIE LEE, poet and author, knocked unconscious by a beer bottle on Sydney Hill, watching Australia v New Zealand, **1974**.

The latest news is that the Hill at Sydney is to be replaced by a stand, so much the better.

E. W. SWANTON, *Follow On*, **1977**.

Taunton

Our spectators went barmy, flung their hats in the air and hit each other about. And they varmers do talk about it to this day.

SAMMY WOODS on Somerset's last ball victory over Surrey at Taunton, **1891**, their first in first-class cricket.

I make the crowd 24; 23 really, because one of them's died there overnight.

TOM YOUNG to R. C. Robertson-Glasgow during a Somerset match at Taunton in the **1920s**.

The Oval

At The Oval, men seem to have rushed away with some zest from their City offices. At Lord's there is a dilettante look, as of men whose work, if any, has yet to come.

REV. JAMES PYCROFT, *Oxford Memories*, **1886**.

Where's the groundsman's hut? If I had a rifle I'd shoot him now.

BILL O'REILLY, Australian spin bowler, during England's 903 for 7, **1938**.

The WACA, Perth

You have to clap yourself on at the WACA.

GARY GILMOUR, on the parochialism of Perth crowds.

Worcester

Look at that, Parkin, 32 overs, 8 maidens, 92 runs, 1 wicket. And they send missionaries to China!

CECIL PARKIN, Lancashire spin bowler, suffering a flat wicket in late **1920s**.

If those boat people want a job, they can come and bowl on this bloody wicket.

NORMAN GIFFORD, Worcestershire spinner, with similar troubles 50 years later, **1978**.

Crowds

The one thing that strikes me about the average crowd – and this is more true of the South than the North – is its ignorance, its startling and fathomless ignorance, of the game in general and the match that is going on in particular.

DUDLEY CAREW. *The Cricketer*, **1928**.

At about two o'clock the sun came out and a great crowd assembled outside the ground. What I hadn't thought of was that two umpires and two captains would sit and wait for so long without making a decision. The crowd broke in, and to save our skins we started to play at 5.20 on a swamp.

ROBERT RYDER, Edgbaston administrator, on England v Australia, **1902**.

And we welcome back listeners to Lord's with the news that steady fighting is continuing in the Long Room and that there will be a further inspection of the pitch when umpire Constant returns from his psychiatrist.

LORD GNOME, in *Private Eye*, after Lord's members involved in scuffles with umpires during rain-delayed Centenary Test, England v Australia, **1980**.

To call a crowd 'a crowd' in Jamaica is a misnomer. It should be called a mob . . . these people still belong to the jungles and forests instead of a civilised society.

SUNIL GAVASKAR, on India's **1976** tour of West Indies in *Sunny Days*.

No sir. Ah didn't coom here t'quell riot. Ah coom t'play cricket.

TED PEATE, refusing Surrey official's request to help stem crowd riot, with England needing only 11 runs to win, v Australia, **1884**.

No, we'll stay. We want another wicket or two this evening.

LEN HUTTON, refusing to leave field for fear of crowd riot, Guyana, MCC tour of West Indies, **1953/4**.

I've seen people hit by bottles and it makes a bloody mess of them.

RAY ILLINGWORTH, England captain, defending decision to take players off the field during crowd trouble at Sydney, **1971**.

Stop the game. We can't see the game. Smoke is getting in our eyes.

G. K. MENON, Indian reporter, striding onto Bombay outfield from press box as stands set alight, India v Australia, **1969**.

On Sundays in particular, we are subjected to the moronic chanting beloved of soccer crowds and decent folk are being driven away by the kind of mindless exhibitionism that has dogged football.

BOB TAYLOR, describing dangers of one-day cricket, in *Standing Up, Standing Back*, **1985**.

A limit to youthful enthusiasm is reached when those delightful young rascals career over the playing area after scalps.

The Cricketer comment on the depredations of autograph hunters at Lord's, Middlesex v Sussex, **1921**.

We must be the only working-class family in Western Australia who have gone ex-directory.

BILL DONNISON, whose son, Gary, was rugby tackled by Australia's Terry Alderman when he invaded the pitch, causing Alderman to damage a shoulder, **1983**.

Official hospitality is an organized conspiracy to prevent the unin-
terrupted watching of cricket, based upon a constant invitation to
'have a drink' or 'meet our sales manager from Slough'.

ROY HATTERSLEY, Labour MP, in the *Guardian*, **1983**.

Don't eat the sausage sandwiches – the sausages are off.

Loudspeaker announcement to schoolboy at Hampshire v Nottinghamshire
match, Portsmouth, **1968**.

'Ere, go easy with the sawdust. You're wasting a full month's
ration of sausage meat.

Worcester spectator, start of Australian tour, **1948**.

Get nearer, point! He won't hurt thee if he hits thee wi't bat!

Yorkshire barracker during typically dour innings by Louis Hall, a nineteenth-
century stonewaller.

Chain t'long beggar up, he's trying to kill 'em.

Bramall Lane spectator, angry at tactics of Fred Spofforth, Australian pace
bowler who claimed to be the fastest in the world, **1889**.

Don't swat those flies Jardine – they're the only friends you've
got in Australia.

Adelaide barracker in Bodyline series, **1932/3**.

Come on Wyatt, get out! We've seen all your strokes except one
– and it'll be a bloody good job when you get that one. That's
sunstroke!

Melbourne barracker to R. E. S. Wyatt, England tour of Australia, **1932/3**.

It serves thee right. Tha should bowl at bloody wickets.

Nelson supporter to Ray Lindwall, Australian quickie, when his début was
marred by dropped slip catches.

Better look in Hansard, Sam.

Sydney spectator to Sam Loxton, member of Victorian parliament and state cricketer, after he had mishit Alan Davidson, **1950s**.

Tyson, why don't you bowl him a piano, perhaps he can play that?

Australian barracker to Frank Tyson, about Neil Harvey, MCC tour, **1954/5**.

Put Harvey on, at least he can throw straight.

Shout from Australian crowd, during throwing allegations against Meckiff, MCC tour, **1958/9**.

Tie ya bat to ya pad Parfitt!

Sydney Hillite's condemnation of Parfitt's tactics against Richie Benaud, Australia v England, **1962/3**.

C'mon Davo, lead him into temptation!

Voice on Sydney Hill, Alan Davidson bowling to Rev. David Sheppard. MCC tour of Australia, **1963**.

Don't forget your pass-out Brownie!

Melbourne spectator, reacting to length of David Brown's run. MCC tour of Australia, **1965/6**.

Bailey, I wish you was a statue and I was a pigeon.

SYDNEY HILLITE, **1954/5** tour.

Come on Brearley, for God's sake; you make Denness look like Don Bradman.

Melbourne barracker. Australia v England, **1978/9**.

Gold Medallion Award for Greatest Winger Would Have To Be Won By J. M. Brearley, Classical Music Lover.

Banner at Melbourne Cricket Ground, England's **1979/80** tour.

Hawke doesn't give a XXX for Aboriginal Land Rights. Thatcher's batting for the Ashes . . . of Democracy in Lambeth. Lambeth Labour Councillors voted in . . . Run Out. It's not cricket.

Banners at Oval Test match, England v Australia, **1985**.

9

They Also Serve

Umpires, Scorers, Groundsmen

Why are the umpires the only two people on a cricket field who aren't going to get grass stains on their knees, the only ones allowed to wear dark trousers?

KATHERINE WHITEHORN, *Observer* columnist.

An umpire should be a man. They are, for the most part, old women.

ROBERT FITZGERALD, *Jerks From Short Leg*, **1866**.

Many umpires are now too old, and their sight not good enough.

SIR HOME GORDON, *The Cricketer*, **1921**.

They are sole judges of all Outs and Ins, of all fair and unfair play, of frivolous delays, of all hurts, whether real or pretended, and are discretionally to allow what time they think proper before ye Game goes on again.

Laws for ye Umpires, **1744**.

When both Umpires shall call Play, three times, 'tis at ye peril of giving ye Game from them that refuse to Play.

Laws for ye Umpires, **1744**.

What goes on in the middle is our business, nothing to do with anybody else.

MERVYN KITCHEN replying to press questions about no-balling Jeff Thomson, **1985**.

'I shall strongly advise you never to accept this supreme hand of authority, in case when match is played between parties each of whom is your friend. You lose your respect in the views of one against whom you express your judgement.

MOHUMMUD ABDULLAH KHAN, *Introduction to Cricket Guide*, **1891**.

Such a duty is still only acceptible (sic) in positions when both the parties take you as their respectible (sic) elder. They think your mistake the very right and pinnicle (sic) of truth, and do never dream of accusition (sic) against your opinion.

As above.

Each and every one of the umpires must avoid using insulting terms or playing on bets with any one of the fielders or persons in general.

As above.

The two umpires undoubtedly have the most wearing and thankless part of the game of the 24 men who take the field in a match. The 'Instructions to Umpires' from *MCC Book, 1920* however have lightened their job to a great extent . . . behind them is the whole weight and strength of the MCC.

F. B. WILSON, *The Cricketer*, **1921**.

In Bombay when England batting there are forty to fifty thousand people shouting every time ball hitting the pad, and in Calcutta, my God, there are ninety thousand people all shouting. But you must concentrate. It is a selfish thing but you must concentrate to save your skin.

SWAROOP KISHEN, Indian Test umpire, in Scyld Berry's *Cricket Wallah*, **1982**.

We have far too much to do in the game these days. You need one eye up your backside.

ARTHUR JEPSON, umpire, bemoaning arrival of fielding circles in one-day cricket, **1981**.

Nowadays, on retiring from the game, the best professional cricketers do not take up umpiring, but prefer to act as coaches at schools or to enter business as athletic and sporting outfitters.

The Cricketer, 'Notes and Comments', **1921**, on umpiring deficiencies.

Amateur players would rather sweep roads or sell newspapers in the street than pretend to be first-class umpires.

CROSS-ARROW, *The Cricketer*, **1927**.

I've always had to count the pennies.

SYD BULLER on an umpire's lot, **1965**.

I have nightmares about having to become an umpire.

JOHN SNOW giving evidence in the High Court on the Packer affair, **1978**.

It's not easy taking up umpiring after being an umpire baiter for over 30 years.

BILL ALLEY, joining umpires list, **1969**.

Most umpires have good memories. If you stuff them once, they'll stuff you good and proper in the end.

ALAN OAKMAN, Warwickshire coach, *From The Nursery End*, **1985**.

See those bloody vultures up there. They're waiting for that bloody umpire. He's got to be dead.

SAM LOXTON, Australian manager, to Pakistan army representatives, when Hanif given 'not out' against Lindwall in Dacca Test.

De MCC proclaim dat dey are not pleased
About some unfair decisions in de West Indies.
Well in de cricket season dese things always happen,
So ah'm askin' you please
Don't put de blame on de West Indies . . .
It happens in England and Australia.
De rules and regulations: no man condemn the umpire's
  decision,
Dats why I'm askin' you please
Don't put the blame on de West Indies.

West Indian calypso, Hutton's MCC tour of West Indies, **1953/4**.

Umpire cursing is previous to Hambledon. Umpire-defiance is older than Dr Grace. He is but a weak-kneed cricketer who *in his heart* approves of the umpire's decisions.

R. C. ROBERTSON-GLASGOW.

The only acceptable form of dissent is a dirty look. And we don't like that.

England Test umpire, **1982**.

I don't understand why, in a democratic society, where government and all the accepted standards in every walk of life are being questioned, umpires should be immune.

ASIF IQBAL, Kent captain, **1982**.

You must be a rogue or a fool.
I suppose I'm a little of both, sir.

Exchange between SIR TIMOTHY O'BRIEN and the umpire at a Cambridgeshire Country house match after the former had been given out caught off his shoulder. According to Buns Thornton, the above version has three expletives deleted.

I couldn't see why I should stand there and have players looking at me as if I were a leper.

TOM BROOKS, retiring as umpire during Australia v England series, **1978/9**.

If they won't accept decisions, there is no point carrying on. Why should I? I'm nearly 60. I don't have to live with this kind of pressure.

ARTHUR FAGG, Test umpire, after West Indies' Rohan Kanhai showed dissent, England v West Indies at Edgbaston, 1973.

I have never come across another umpire so full of his own importance, so stubborn, lacking in humour, unreasonable, and utterly unable to distinguish between a delivery short of a length which rises around the height of the rib-cage and a genuine bouncer which goes through head high, as Lou Rowan.

JOHN SNOW, *Cricket Rebel*, 1976.

You'll never die wondering, son.

CEC PEPPER, umpire, reacting to numerous lbw appeals from Ashley Mallett, Australian spin bowler, 1968.

As God is my witness!

Alex Skelding, umpire, awarding a hat-trick of lbw decisions to Yorkshire's Horace Fisher v Somerset at Scarborough, 1932.

He's out and we've won the championship!

Umpire and Welshman DAI DAVIES, giving decision as John Clay took wicket which gave Glamorgan their first county championship success, 1948.

Doubt? When I'm umpiring, there's never any doubt!

FRANK CHESTER, asked when he gave a batsman the benefit of the doubt.

Batsmen seem to be getting away with lbw appeals which makes me wonder about the umpires. It would be only human, if every critical decision is to be played back endlessly, for them to opt for less controversy and aggravation. I pray that our umpires are not becoming 'Not Outers'.

SIR LEN HUTTON on the effect of TV coverage in 1985, England v Australia series.

The 'Outer' – large of frame, rubicund of countenance, who drinks pints and eats vastly, is a gay, carefree fellow who, in his playing days, was a fast bowler and who now has only to hear somebody in the crowd clear his throat for his finger to shoot aloft.

MICHAEL STEVENSON in *The Cricketer*, **1963**.

The 'Not Outer' . . . is small, wizened, misanthropic, drinks half-shandies and eats sparingly.

MICHAEL STEVENSON, as above.

And that, gentlemen, concludes the entertainment for the day.

ALEX SKELDING, umpire, catchphrase.

Umpiring at the top now is full of comedians and gimmicks. In the old days there used to be men you could respect.

CEC PEPPER, resigning from first-class umpire's list, **1980**.

Ian sent it me and he wants me to wear it in the Test. How could I? It would be advertising wouldn't it?

DICKIE BIRD, Test umpire, after receiving a Botham fedora through the post, **1985**.

Before a series with the West Indies starts I have a box of caps sent from Luton in the sure knowledge I am going to lose one or two.

DICKIE BIRD, Test umpire, in *That's Out*, **1985**.

I reckon I sent two fans to hospital at the end of the England-New Zealand game at The Oval. I worked on a dockside for 30 years and know how to dish it out if I need to.

DON OSLEAR, Test umpire, after repelling pitch invaders with a stump at Old Trafford, **1983**.

Derek Underwood could never bowl at my end – he could not get round me.

SWAROOP KISHEN, heavyweight Indian Test umpire, admission to Dickie Bird (from *That's Out*, **1985**).

Here's three ha'pence. Buy a paper and find out the score.

ALEX SKELDING, umpire, at odds with scoreboard operators in a county match.

Slow down Mr Gooch, I can't keep up with you.

Electronic scoreboard appeal to Graham Gooch, during Essex v West Indies floodlit match at Chelsea FC, **1980**.

There was a social prejudice against the scorer who was a descendant of the baggage man.

VIC ISAACS, Hampshire scorer and statistician, quoted in *A Walk To The Wicket* by Ted Dexter and David Lemmon, **1985**.

The scientists fail us . . . they cannot do anything to supply men who are born to be groundsmen.

COLIN COWDREY, from *MCC*, **1976**.

It is a remarkable fact that every time a side has a bad innings it is the wicket that is blamed – never the player.

The Groundsman, **1958**.

Thank God Nasser has taken over the Suez Canal. Otherwise, I'd have been plastered over every front page like Marilyn Monroe.

BERT FLACK, Old Trafford groundsman, after Laker's 19 wickets for England against Australia, **1956**.

There should have been a last line of defence during the war. It would have been made up entirely of the more officious breed of cricket stewards. If Hitler had tried to invade these shores he would have been met by a short, stout man in a white coat who would have said: 'I don't care who you are, you're not coming in here unless you're a member.'

RAY EAST, in *A Funny Turn*, **1983**.

They sure do like their tea, these Englishmen.

Scottish tannoy announcer, as umpire Dickie Bird called two tea intervals,
Scotland v Yorkshire, Benson and Hedges Cup, **1984**.

Don't forget tonight's social evening in aid of the Clive Rice
Memorial Fund.

Worksop tannoy announcer, Notts v Yorkshire, **1985**. It was for Rice's benefit.

The Press

. . . and the press box creaking, stretching,
fidgeting, vulture-like waits
with the sound of sharpening carbon claws
for the fresh carcass of play.

JOHN SNOW, from Lord's Test, in *Moments and Thoughts*, **1973**.

I'm here to propose the toast to the sportswriters. It's up to you
whether you stand up or not.

FRED TRUEMAN, Sportswriters Association Dinner, **1964**.

Journalism and batting are not so different . . . a few good strokes
are often better remembered than all the padding in between.

TED DEXTER, **1974**.

BRITISH AIRWAYS STEWARD: Would you like me to take anything
home for you?
BOB WILLIS: Yes, 34 journalists and two camera crews.

England's tour of West Indies, **1986**.

English first-class cricket has been played for the benefit of the
cricket writers and the newspapers . . . most writers know the
parlous state of county cricket, yet they had to support it, to
ensure it survived to support them. They had a vested interest in
the system which existed.

ANDREW CARO, former WSC managing director on press's hostile reaction to
Packer Circus. *Wisden Cricket Monthly*, **1980**.

I suppose we are right in giving so much space to cricket, though I have been told by those who have been to see them that most of the county matches are very poorly attended, and chiefly by old men.

LORD NORTHCLIFFE, owner of *The Times*, **1919**.

I will never be accepted by the snob press.

RAY ILLINGWORTH, **1973**.

Most cricket critics, who have more power than any other writers in sport, would see Chairman Mao as British Prime Minister before they would give Boycott the vote as England captain.

IAN WOOLDRIDGE, *Daily Mail*.

The press wanted my reaction to the Yorkshire decision and when I refused to comment . . . they did what the press usually do. They became cutting and critical, as if it was my job to fill their columns for them. They smile and then they stab – and they think the next time they come along for a comment you are going to forget the wounding things they write and obligingly talk to them.

GEOFFREY BOYCOTT, on his sacking as Yorkshire captain, in *Put to the Test*, **1979**.

During these tours the captain is interviewed by reporters more or less all day, sometimes early in the morning when I was in my bath. It is policy to receive them even with a bath towel, because if you don't, they will report you just the same, only it would be their idea of things, not mine.

E. J. METCALFE, describing Colonel Greenway's tour to Philadelphia, **1913**, in *The Cricketer*, **1932**.

I knew I could never be a 'real' newspaper journalist – it was such a difficult job to be hail-fellow-well-met-what's-yours-old-boy in private life and next day have to scalpel-slash a reputation in public print.

FRANK KEATING, *Another Bloody Day in Paradise*, **1981**.

I do know that I wouldn't enjoy making my living by criticising my former colleagues.

BOB WILLIS, **1983**.

I have grown to trust and like several of the cricket writers. Equally, there are some I trust but don't like, others I like but don't trust and the occasional individual I neither like nor trust.

BOB WILLIS, *The Captain's Diary*, **1983**.

When you have to spend the tour in your hotel room so you're not stitched up, there's something wrong.

IAN BOTHAM, England's tour of West Indies, **1986**.

One would suppose that the invasion of publicity and the general mateyness of radio and press would have tended to produce something like swollen-headedness in the prominent players. But one would be in error. The tendency, so far as one can see, is for publicity to produce more and more modesty of demeanour.

C. B. FRY, *The Cricketer*, **1955**.

Young man, my contract with the *Daily Mail* is so tight that I can't even tell you the time of day.

DON BRADMAN, to Don Mosey, young reporter, **1953**.

Gower's efforts to win the support of Botham were based exclusively on joining the Botham-Lamb bollocks-to-the-media campaign.

DON MOSEY, *The Best Job In The World*, **1985**.

Criticism is not new; it has not been dreamed up specially for this highly-sensitive bunch of prima donnas who represent the Establishment of the England Test side in this era.

DON MOSEY, as above.

It may be hoped that the MCC will in future remove their edict, which does not permit a cricketer on tour abroad to write on that tour, and appoint one of the team, who can be trusted not to commit faux pas, to write descriptions of the matches.

The Cricketer, on lack of news of West Indies tour, **1926**.

One of the problems is that England players are saying one thing to a reporter one day, and another in their ghosted columns the next.

Cricket journalist, on England players writing ghosted columns on West Indies tour, **1976**.

My ghost is writing rubbish.

England player on West Indies tour, **1986**.

In the dog-eat-dog ethos of freelance journalism, there seems little place for those who are not naturally carnivorous.

MICHAEL STEVENSON explaining his decision to go back to teaching. *The Cricketer*, **1982**.

One gets used to the abysmal ignorance of some colleagues, to whom any slip catch has resulted from 'an outswinger' and any shot which ends in the third man area is 'a cut'.

STEVENSON on his erstwhile colleagues in the press box, **1982**.

These experts are spoiling the market for the others. They are no journalists – the mere writing of articles does not make one a journalist. You have to go through the mill, then develop specialisation. Anyway, no cricketer I have ever known was able to write well.

ALEX BANNISTER, *Daily Mail* correspondent.

Ted Dexter is to journalism what Danny La Rue is to Rugby League.

MICHAEL PARKINSON.

How do you spell 'repertoire' mate?

IAN CHAPPELL, freshly into press box, Centenary Test, **1980**.

I'm afraid I shall be a bit out of touch with the general chorus of press commentators on the game. They are all so solemn. They deliver judgements almost legal, as though in chambers.

SIR NEVILLE CARDUS, embarking upon his 51st season as cricket writer, **1970**.

It's plastic-cupped, can-I-borrow-your-phone press boxes. When we talk it's talk of mortgages. 'Whose turn, old boy?' means 'Get out your Thermos.' You can never borrow a Biro, they've only got fountain pens. When play gets going, it's eyes down into Wisden.

FRANK KEATING on life in cricket press boxes, **1974**.

British Telecom: their finger on the button? My hands round their throat!

MARTIN SEARBY, freelance journalist, in live BBC broadcast on new radio phone, **1985**.

By 2000 the TV camera will be everywhere: dressing room, hotel and bathroom. I visualise the newsman's mania for live human action and reaction breaking all the bounds of privacy and decency.

TONY LEWIS, **1969**.

One viewer told me the other day that listening to my old mate Jim Laker and his new sidekick Bob Willis was better than taking two Mogadon.

FRED TRUEMAN on TV commentators, **1985**.

If anybody had told me I was one day destined to make a reputation as a writer on cricket I should have felt hurt.

NEVILLE CARDUS, *Autobiography*, **1947**.

Ah reckon, Mr Cardus, tha's invented me.

EMMOTT ROBINSON.

Ah'd like to bowl at bugger soom da-ay.

DICK TYLDESLEY, Lancashire batsman, about Neville Cardus, quoted in Cardus's *Autobiography*, **1947**.

It is doubtful whether anyone, unwittingly, has done more harm to the game than Cardus. No doubt unconsciously, Cardus conde-scended to cricket, encapsulating social attitudes that were unreal even when he started watching it. Cricket writers deal in stereo-types, stereotypes with regional and social overtones – Ranji, the wily Oriental, Tyldesley the honest yoeman, MacLaren, the lordly aristo. On the one hand the gents, on the other, lovable but inarticulate, full of character and simple humour, possessed of a God-given gift they did not rightly understand – the professionals.

NICHOLAS RICHARDSON, *New Society*, **1975**.

But my dear chap, it's the spirit of the thing that counts. Often when I quoted a player he may not literally have said those things. But he'd have liked to.

NEVILLE CARDUS.

Neville Cardus would go crazy if he had to spend half an hour with a commercial traveller: I know, because I introduced him to one a few years ago.

ARTHUR MAILEY.

John Arlott has been that rarity, a man respected by the players as much as the public . . . somehow Arlott's presence made you feel cricket was in good hands.

BRIAN BRAIN. *Another Day, Another Match*, **1981**.

My dad's only claim to sporting fame was that he went to school with John Arlott.

GRAHAM ROOPE (Surrey, England), **1970s**.

No-one could be utterly dull in the presence of Katherine, Duchess of Kent.

E. W. SWANTON.

BRING BACK WARD!

The *Sun*, northern edition, 16th August **1974**.

BRING BACK SNOW!

The *Sun*, southern edition, 16th August **1974**.

10
Showing the Flag

Touring

What will dear mother say when she sees I have travelled 1,134 miles to be bowled out first ball?

CHARLES WRIGHT, Lord Hawke's XI v Chicago, **1896**.

Nay, I make nowt of it. I'd rather be at Lascelles Hall where I was reared.

EPHRAIM LOCKWOOD, on tour with Daft's team, at Niagara Falls.

At Peshawar I stayed with a cousin of Jardine. On the first morning we parted on the doorstep. I to play cricket, he to settle a tribal war.

LORD LIONEL TENNYSON, describing **1937/8** tour of India.

First came your white dinner jacket, then your black dinner jacket, then your tails. Fourth was your topee, fifth your sports jacket and sixth your rifle. After that, if you had room, you might cram in some cricket equipment.

COLIN COWDREY, on manner of early tours to India, in *MCC*, **1976**.

It's 8.30 on a Friday night; what am I doing in Ahmedabad?

GRAEME FOWLER, England's tour of India **1984**, in Vic Marks's *Marks out of Eleven*, 1985.

Pakistan days are long when you wake up at 4 a.m.

BOB WILLIS, *The Captain's Diary*, **1983**.

Excuse me, I'm from the IRA, could you direct me towards the English dressing room, please?

GRAHAM MORRIS, photographer, testing Indian security arrangements after assassination of Mrs Gandhi, Bombay Test, **1984**.

Since the England players arrived on 31st October, India had the assassination of its Prime Minister and a British diplomat 24 hours after he entertained us, thousands of deaths in communal slaughter, the Bhopal disaster, the world's most elaborate democratic exercise and a spy scandal. One morning in New Zealand the main item on the morning news concerned a fisherman trying to land a large marlin.

MATTHEW ENGEL, the *Guardian*, **1985**.

Not everyone . . . is gifted with the temperament and also, may I add, stomach of Albert Trott, to whom everything came alike, fair weather and foul, good food or no food, sleep or no sleep; it was all the same to him – an ideal professor for a tour.

FRANK MITCHELL.

Did I find Test tours too strenuous? The very question is sacriligious.

ARTHUR MAILEY.

'A vulgar little thing, but she lives abundantly' remarked Budge Firth, that twentieth century Pickwick, as he watched with benevolent amusement a certain lady playing deck-tennis somewhere between Trafalgar and Corunna. Which criticism . . . may aptly be said to describe the Cryptics' tour in Gibraltar.

R. C. ROBERTSON-GLASGOW, *The Cricketer*, **1927**.

The contrast between the civilian life of the ordinary Australian cricketer and his existence as a touring Test player is fantastic. I cannot think of one of my contemporaries who was fabulous enough to live at a decent hotel or travel a hundred miles in luxury.

ARTHUR MAILEY.

It was far beyond my imagination . . . that one day a manservant would collect six sets of my flannels and bring them back fastidiously laundered next morning. Every time this happened my mind went back to a leaking tub in a Waterloo backyard, and this one thought seemed to be a basis for every other set of comparative circumstances in my Test career.

ARTHUR MAILEY.

You fellows should never have played cricket if you hate it so much! If I were Sid Smith (the Australian manager) I'd bundle you moaning cows off home straight away.

EDGAR MAYNE to his discontented team mates at The Oval during the **1921** Australian tour (quoted by Arthur Mailey).

It usually happens that those who play least do most of the complaining about the strain of being on tour and flop about the dressing-room like marathon runners drained of their last tincture of energy. But let somebody suggest a game of golf and those immobile sufferers suddenly take a new lease of life.

ARTHUR MAILEY.

We need players who are prepared to slug it out for the whole tour.

Australian captain ALLAN BORDER after his side's collapse in the last two tests of the **1985** tour.

I persuaded them that to take a towel out to Viv Richards or to dry Clive Lloyd's socks is as good as scoring 20 or 30.

SENATOR WES HALL, West Indies manager, on how he kept the young players happy when not playing on tour of Australia, **1984/5**.

The leading cricketers in this country play virtually six days a
week throughout the home season, including, in many cases, five
Test matches, and are called upon to tour abroad two out of three
winters. They are thus subjected to considerable strain and are
separated from their families for long periods. The county clubs
unreservedly support MCC's view that, both in the personal interests of the players, and for the maintenance of the standard of
,play in county and international cricket, the duration of the longer
MCC tours must be curtailed.

MCC statement, **1958**.

A two months tour, containing five full Test matches, is a fresh
approach to international cricket, and if the experiment is
successful could be accepted as a blueprint for future programmes.
Already MCC are looking into the prospects of fitting two tours
into the English summer. It is all part of the 'jet' age.

The Cricketer, editorial, **1963**.

Three to six months of constant packing and unpacking, living out
of suitcases with home a succession of impersonal hotel rooms,
some good, some bad, the majority indifferent. The tourist's life
is in the open, with every move made under the spotlight of
publicity. The television lens watches everything on the field, the
curious eyes of strangers watch in hotels and streets, at receptions,
cocktail parties and a succession of dinners. The moments of
complete freedom are few and far between.

JOHN SNOW, *Cricket Rebel*, **1976**.

I don't go along with the argument that the players are under too
much pressure and spending too much time away from home.
They want to make big money out of the game – well the only
way to do so is to tour and play. Players cannot expect to sit on
their backsides and be paid for just being Test cricketers. They
must work at their profession if that is the profession they want.

BOBBY SIMPSON, former Australian captain, in *Howzat*, **1980**.

You would think this English Test team was in a holiday camp. Their dining room has high chairs for the players' children and on mornings of tough Tests there are England's heroes popping cornflakes into their youngsters' mouths. In Brisbane and Sydney it was absurd to call these men with bats 'batsmen': they were week-kneed imposters.

KEITH MILLER, former Australian all-rounder, *Daily Express* on the Denness tour, **1974/5**.

Lord Hawke, had he been asked about it, might have taken the same view as I do about having families on tour. It is no more the place for them than a trench on the Somme.

JOHN WOODCOCK, *The Times*, MCC tour of Australia, **1975**.

Our hotels were turned into kindergartens.

BOB TAYLOR, in *Standing Up, Standing Back*, on presence of wives and children on England's Australian tour, **1974/5**.

Wives and families must never tour again with players . . . there is little team spirit and even less fight. Women and children come first for these players who have families. To hell with the pride of England seems to be their motto.

KEITH MILLER, former Australian all-rounder, in *Daily Express*, **1975**.

What this pitch wants is ten minutes of the heavy roller.

JOHN WISDEN on Atlantic, **1859**.
TOM EMMETT on Bay of Biscay, **1876**.

OCTOBER 6: Beautiful morning, sea smooth. Sports tournament commenced. I got beaten in the first round of peg quoits by Fielder. Had very good game deck cricket after tea. Wrote letters and sent postcards. Went to concert in second-class saloon. Passed the Isle of Crete. Saw partial eclipse of the moon. Rather damp atmosphere at night. Dancing on first-class deck. Ship's run: 363 miles.

ALBERT RELF, professional all-rounder, excerpt from diary of MCC's first tour of Australia, **1903/4**.

The tour from start to finish involving two long sea voyages, one, from Southampton to Buenos Aires, of 6,000 miles, and the other, from Valparaiso via the Panama canal, to Plymouth, of 9,000 miles, while the distance covered by railway totalled quite 3,000 miles. Surely no cricket team ever saw so much 'cities and men' in the course of 3 months.

PELHAM WARNER on the MCC tour of South America, **1926/7** (from *The Cricketer*).

We had free passes over the railways, and special trains of the most luxurious type carried us to Concordia, to Rosario, to Mar del Plata – the Trouville of Argentina – with its superb sea-bathing, golf links and Casino.

PELHAM WARNER, as above.

The match in Rosario was spoilt by the weather . . . but that did not alter the fact that P. F. Warner was only able to field 9 men, which was a great disappointment to Rosario as well as to the Argentine Cricket Association.

E. W. S. THOMSON on Warner's MCC tour of South America, **1927**.

It is no small matter to organise the visit of an MCC team, and the Argentine Cricket Association, after having raised some £3,000 to defray expenses, should have felt perfectly secure on the point that there was no shortage of players. The invitation issued was for 14 men with all expenses paid, and yet the MCC would not sanction more than 12 players.

E. W. S. THOMSON.

Other points of interest during the passage were the erection of a cricket-net where Bettington alone, owing to the senile lowness of his deliveries, was able to bowl without barking his knuckles on the deck above.

R. C. ROBERTSON-GLASGOW, Cryptics tour of Gibraltar, **1927**.

New Year's Eve was spent somewhere over Uruguay on a DC6, conducted in seasonal community singing by a Roman Catholic priest who used a champagne glass for a baton.

D. R. W. SILK on the MCC tour of Brazil and Argentina, **1958/9**.

Two of the team slept in their cars with windows tightly shut as they had heard that mambas could jump, while the remainder removed what they could of the layers of light brown dust from the day's journey and dozed fitfully in the lounge.

Romany's tour of South Africa, **1960/61**, the first by a club side as reported in *The Cricketer*.

Why are we going to this confounded place? Most likely when we get there they (the Boers) will fire at us on the cricket field.

Un-named member (probably Charles Wright) of Lord Hawke's touring team in South Africa on forthcoming visit to Johannesburg in the aftermath of the Jameson Raid.

We got invitations to coon dances, and on the card 'T.W.B.F.'. On asking what it meant we were informed 'there would be fun' – and there was.

SAMMY WOODS on Arthur Priestley's tour to West Indies, **1897**.

At about four o'clock in the afternoon the engine became 'pumped' and a long halt was made while the machinery was overhauled. The natives, who were (physically) rather a poor looking lot, collected round the team, and a sort of indaba was held by Lord Hawke outside the saloon. This was a splendid chance for the photographers of the team, and one fine nigger, for the magnificent sum of a 'tickey' (3d), formed the centre-piece of a group which included most of the professionals.

PELHAM WARNER in *Cricket in Many Climes* describing Lord Hawke's tour of South Africa **1908**, going up country by train to Bulawayo.

(Who will forget) 'Jacko Hobbo', the dressing-room attendant in the pavilion, a Chesterfield in manners, ever ready with 'whiskey soda' or 'gin tonic' to quench the thirst which so easily arises in that scorching and often damp heat.

PELHAM WARNER on Buenos Aires during MCC tour of South America, **1926/7**.

From the Ambassador and Lady Wallinger down to the grinning lift-boy at the Miramar Hotel on Copacabana, the kindness and friendship shown us had positively glowed.

D. R. W. SILK, Brazil, **1958/9**.

After they were out, Waddy and certain others decided to make a tour of the large Roman Catholic cemetery which adjoined the field. They were scaling a wall, when a policeman sprang up and levelled a firearm at Waddy's head. However, conversation and a judicious use of the ever-ready port bottle saved the situation.

Cryptics' tour in Portugal, *The Cricketer*, **1925**.

Wednesday was nominally a free morning in which we were encouraged to visit a wine lodge and also to see how the Portuguese lived. We had often pondered on this latter subject after seeing some of them driving cars in Lisbon, but it was the former that attracted our attentions for the whole morning.

Report on Cryptics' tour of Portugal, **1961** in *The Cricketer*.

We had dined well at the Kimberley Club, and the old Boer told me not to drink too much of the milk. Unfortunately I had done so. The result was that in less time than it takes to relate, I was vomiting little pieces of iced milk, which made my throat so bad I couldn't speak for three days – shows we must take advice in strange countries.

SAMMY WOODS on Lord Hawke's tour to South Africa.

At St Anne's Bay there was not anyone at the place where we put up who could mix cocktails, a most essential drink in that country to make one alive before breakfast and before dinner. 'Little Reds' and 'Little Greens' they are called.

SAMMY WOODS on Arthur Priestley's tour to the West Indies, **1897**.

I made them (cocktails) for the team before breakfast. I don't know what ingredients I mixed with them, still I remember we had to borrow two substitutes at 12 o'clock when we started play.

SAMMY WOODS.

Easter Sunday found some in bed till noon, and others attending the military parade service. After which there set out a grand motor expedition on a circular tour . . . which, owing to the fact that our first and last halt was a certain wayside inn, might more aptly be called a concentric tour.

R. C. ROBERTSON-GLASGOW, Cryptics' tour of Gibraltar, 1927.

Christmas Day was a very happy open-air affair – wonderful cold turkey, asparagus, salads and the appropriate liquid accompaniments on the lawn followed by tennis, swimming and other forms of exercise.

Romany's tour of South Africa, 1960/61.

The Duke had put one or two whisky-and-sodas away so was quite easy to get along with.

PAUL GIBB, diary account of Duke of Gloucester's meeting with Australian and MCC teams, Melbourne, 1946/7 tour.

You can't muck around with eggs and you can't muck around with chips.

KEN BARRINGTON, explaining his eating habits in India, quoted in Frank Keating's *Another Bloody Day in Paradise*, 1981.

The Church and the Navy were both represented at dinner in our hotel that night; but the navy alone (Lieutenant Allison) accompanied us to a somewhat Neronian evening at the R. A. Mess where, if my memory serves me aright, at least one billiard ball passed out of a closed window.

R. C. ROBERTSON-GLASGOW Cryptics' tour of Gibraltar, 1927.

The formation of a players' committee to deal with the social engagements of the team will, I hope, prevent a repetition of some unfortunate 'incidents' last year, when invitations, accepted for the players, were either totally ignored or treated in a 'casual Australian' manner that must have been intensely irritating to their hosts.

CLEM HILL former Australian captain, in *The Cricketer*, 1927.

We tarried long after the sun had set ... at ... Manheim, Philadelphia, where, after a bath in a scented swimming pool, we dressed and met beautiful women with whom we danced in the club ballroom or sipped champagne on the terraces.

ARTHUR MAILEY.

Cricket in Philadelphia took me to far greater imaginative heights than nine Test wickets in Melbourne or 'ten for 66' against Gloucester in 1921.

ARTHUR MAILEY.

Who will forget Hurlingham, that Paradise of Country Clubs – or the dance there on New Year's Eve – tell it not in Gath, publish it not in Askalon – in the middle of the first Argentina match.

PELHAM WARNER on the MCC tour of South America, **1926/7** (from *The Cricketer*).

At Rio we stayed a night at the Capacabana (sic) Hotel, where we danced on a glass floor, won money at the Casino, and bathed in a glittering sea.

PELHAM WARNER on the MCC tour of South America, **1926/7**.

We were made members of all the clubs – even of the exclusive Jockey Club at Buenos Aires – with its magnificent house, marble staircase, priceless pictures, open-air restaurant, library, squash racquet court, swimming and Turkish baths.

PELHAM WARNER.

It rained from Tuesday to Thursday and cricket was out of the question. There was a racket court, however ... There was climbing, a whole day of it, over the Rock in a steady downpour led by an undaunted Sergeant. There was golf at Campo Mento, on the strip of land that joins Gibraltar to Spain, in the course of which Bettington menaced a diminutive caddie with a rather large niblick, for reasons that could only be attributed to liver.

R. C. ROBERTSON-GLASGOW on the expeditions of players on their days off from the Cryptics' tour of Gibraltar, **1927**.

Those of us who remained on the bridge of cricket throughout the four months were, to some extent, compensated by the return of Hough and Maitland from Tangier, falsely jocular and strangely uncommunicative about anything except a night's sleep of two hours followed by a grim passage in a steam-launch to catch their boat at six in the morning.

R. C. ROBERTSON-GLASGOW.

Not a single game was played within the British Empire – another proof that cricket has set a girdle round the earth.

PELHAM WARNER, South America, **1926/7**.

From Monte Video on the Atlantic to Lima on the Pacific, the MCC flag was seen, and it was remarked by Sir Hilary Leng . . . at the Jockey Club at Buenos Aires we were 'not only ambassadors of cricket, but of Empire'.

PELHAM WARNER.

That was a good 'un for a trial ball.

CHARLES WRIGHT to bowler after being bowled comprehensively first ball, Lord Hawke's XI v Chicago. The ploy did not work.

I have from the very outset regarded these tours primarily as imperial enterprises, tending to cement friendship between the Mother Country and her Dominions. Players . . . should not be chosen for their cricket qualities alone. They must be men of good character, high principle, easy of address, and in every personal sense worthy of representing their country in all circumstances, irrespective of their work on the field.

SIR FREDERICK TOONE, three-time manager of Australia, in *Wisden*, **1930**.

Silk spread the field out defensively and this upset Toronto completely. What had nearly been a convincing victory for the local side had been turned into a frustrating draw by Silk's calm tactics.

M. H. BUSHBY's report on the MCC tour of Canada, **1959** (from *The Cricketer*).

It was not only very hot, with a temperature, on occasions, of 100 deg. in the shade, but it was often a damp heat, and the health, and, consequently, the form of several members of the side suffered.

PELHAM WARNER, South America, **1926/7**.

Well Bob, this must be the worst English team ever to reach these shores?

Bob Willis's first question on arriving with England team for tour of Australia, **1982**.

11
Tribes Without the Law

Yorkshiremen, Australians and Others

I know plenty of professionals whom I would delight to have as guests in my own home, but I am afraid I cannot say the same thing about most of the Australians I have met.

A. W. CARR (Nottinghamshire, England) in the **1930s** in *Cricket With The Lid Off*. **1935**

I have on occasions taken a quite reasonable dislike to the Australians.

TED DEXTER, **1972**.

In all this Australian team there are barely one or two who would be accepted as public school men.

C. B. FRY, then a journalist, on the **1938** Australians.

The only time an Australian walks is when his car runs out of petrol.

BARRY RICHARDS, **1980**.

To take the most charitable view of the position, the behaviour of Australian crowds at its best, when judged by the standards accepted in the rest of the world, is not naturally good.

D. R. JARDINE after the Bodyline tour.

I never dreamed that an English crowd would find comedy in Australian batting.

ARTHUR MAILEY on the Old Trafford crowd's response to Mackay's shot against Laker, **1956**.

When you come back from Australia, you feel you've been in Vietnam.

GLENN TURNER, New Zealand batsman, **1983**.

The air is thick with bad language, the cheating is on a massive scale and the threatening gestures are rife.

BOB TAYLOR, in *Standing Up, Standing Back*, on attitudes in Sydney schools cricket, **1985**.

I don't think very much of their play but they're a wonderful lot of drinking men.

ROGER IDDISON, member of England's first tour to Australia, on the Australian characteristics, **1861/2**.

If you ever come to England and your bowlers are as good there as they are here, you will make a name for yourselves.

W. G. GRACE, on tour of Australia, **1873**.

If the Australians did not make cricket their profession in their native land, they most decidedly did when they came to this country; for all who had anything to do with them soon found out how keen they were about '£ s d'.

Lillywhite's Cricketers' Companion on Australian 'amateurs', **1880**.

Unconsciously, and perhaps without any suspicion on their part that such is the case, the Australians have seriously and perceptibly aggravated the symptoms of a commercial spirit in cricket.

Lillywhite's Cricketers' Companion, **1882**, on the Australian tour. The Australians played 38 matches but refused to play before noon or after 6pm.

The visits of the two Australian XI's to England may be held responsible for the sudden and extraordinary change which took place in the bearing of professionals who had previously comported themselves most becomingly.

Lillywhite's Cricketers' Companion, **1882**.

Bookmakers seem to be among the chief patrons of the game, as is, perhaps, not unnatural where the line between gentlemen and players is almost non-existent to the native English eye. The Australians are excellent cricketers . . . but the colony does not possess the class of gentlemen of leisure who can afford to give up the time and trouble to organizing the pastime and keeping up its moral and social tone.

First issue of *Cricket*, **1882**, on Australian game.

I'm responsible for this storm and there will be more such storms until the Australians pay their debts.

DORIS MUNDAY, in phone call to Lord's, claiming she had used powers of occult to cause hailstones to fall in June, because she had not been paid for breaking drought in Australia, **1968**.

I always carried powdered resin in my pocket and when the umpire wasn't looking lifted the seam for Jack Gregory and Ted McDonald.

ARTHUR MAILEY, *10 for 66 and All That*.

This prohibition against resin was the more unreasonable in that wicket-keepers were still allowed to use bird-lime on their gloves. Whenever I ran out of resin I used to spend a good part of the day shaking hands with Bert Oldfield, our 'keeper.

ARTHUR MAILEY, *10 for 66 and All That*.

Stay in the slips. You've got a better chance of lifting the seams for Jack (Gregory) and Stork (Hendry) there.

HERBY COLLINS to Arthur Mailey when the latter asked to move to the covers after dropping a catch.

I once saw a bowler in Australia thunder to the wicket and bowl a flat-out underarm at the batsman. No warning given. Quite right, too. In my profession you have to mystify the enemy.

FIELD MARSHAL VISCOUNT MONTGOMERY.

We sat in the Windsor Hotel until two in the morning evolving attacking schemes, drawing field placings, thinking of all manner of distractions such as loose bowling sleeves *à la* Ramadhin, bowlers wearing red caps designed like cricket balls; and even our captain Collins, a man with a rich appreciation of the manly old game, lowered his ideals to such a state that he suggested in all seriousness an ordinary, under-arm 'grubber'.

ARTHUR MAILEY on the Australian team's desperation after Hobbs and Sutcliffe had batted all day in **1924/5**. The next day Mailey bowled Hobbs first ball with a full toss!

It was an act of cowardice and I consider it appropriate that the Australians were wearing yellow.

ROBERT MULDOON, New Zealand Prime Minister, on Trevor Chappell's underarm delivery with six needed to win off the final ball, Melbourne, **1981**.

Fair dinkum, Greg, how much pride do you sacrifice to win 35,000 dollars?

IAN CHAPPELL, **1981** (his brother Greg was captain).

When I was a kid, I was always told the game's not over until the last ball is **bowled**.

DOUG WALTERS, on the same incident.

You get the impression the Laws of the game are written on a dollar note.

D. J. CAMERON, *New Zealand Herald*, on same incident, **1981**.

ROD MARSH: Plan A is to fight fire with fire . . . in others words, try to crack a few skulls.
GREG CHAPPELL: No, Rod, it's beers that are for cracking, heads are for using thoughtfully.

The Australian wicket-keeper's plan to beat the West Indies is rejected by his captain, **1984**.

We don't play this game for fun.

WILFRED RHODES.

We shake hands on t' first morning and say: 'How do?'; then we say nowt for three days, but: 'How's that?'.

ROY KILNER on **1920s** Lancashire v Yorkshire matches. Also ascribed to Emmott Robinson.

Cricket was never made for any championship . . . Cricket's a game, not a competition.

GEORGE HIRST.

What we want in Yarksheer and Lankysheer matches is 'fair do's' – no umpires, and honest cheatin' all round . . .

ROY KILNER, Yorkshire all-rounder, on Roses matches (quoted in Neville Cardus's *Autobiography*, **1947**).

We'll get 'em in singles.

GEORGE HIRST to Wilfred Rhodes (apocryphal), last-wicket stand of 15 for England to beat Australia at The Oval, **1902**.

Nice night for it, eh?

GRAHAM STEVENSON, to Australian captain Ian Chappell, joining his Yorkshire team-mate David Bairstow, for match-winning partnership in Sydney floodlit match, **1981**.

Evening lad. We can piss this y'know.

BAIRSTOW to Stevenson in the same match.

Don't tell me his average or his top score at Trent Bridge. How many runs, how many wickets did he get against Yorkshire?

D. R. JARDINE's standard for judging potential Test cricketers.

The trouble with you damn Yorkshiremen is that you are only interested in playing this game to win.

Former England captain to Fred Trueman during tour of Australia.

It is the bugbear of Yorkshiremen that they always feel that they have to behave like Yorkshiremen, or like their fixed belief in what a Yorkshireman should be: tough, ruthless, brave, mean.

ALAN GIBSON in The Cricketer, 1978.

Gerrup, tha's makin' an exhibition o' thiself.

ARTHUR 'TICKER' MITCHELL to Yorkshire colleague Ellis Robinson after spectacular diving catch.

The Yorkshire County Cricket Club has behaved like the Labour Party in its worst periods. Every time there's a little dispute, everybody attacks each other in public.

ROY HATTERSLEY, Labour Party politician, 1983.

It is not likely to be possible to pass fair judgement on the cricketers of Yorkshire, qua cricketers, until the club has undergone radical heart surgery.

JOHN ARLOTT, 1984.

Someone born within the sound of Bill Bowes.

MIKE CAREY, Daily Telegraph, definition of a Yorkshireman.

Yorkshire sacked me because I refused to accept the authority of the quite hopeless old man appointed captain.

JOHNNY WARDLE, after sacking by Yorkshire, 1958.

The atmosphere in the once all-conquering Yorkshire has got worse and worse, both on and off the field . . . and the faults in the committee room are as much a cause of Yorkshire's lowly position as the shortcomings on the field.

JOHNNY WARDLE, the *Daily Mail*, **1958**.

I see that I'm being accused now of breaking my contract by writing for *The Daily Mail*. What contract? All I've ever been given was a book of rules and regulations.

JOHNNY WARDLE.

For years I have said that Yorkshire is run by a lot of people who think their old-fashioned methods are good enough to cope with modern cricket. A rot has set in with Yorkshire. And it's eating away the greatest county club in the world.

JOHNNY WARDLE.

Maybe I swore with justification. Often they were the sort of catches that could have been taken comfortably had the offender been in bed at the same time as I was.

JOHNNY WARDLE, accused by Clifford Hesketh, chairman of Yorkshire's selection committee, of bad language towards team-mates, **1958**.

He may be good enough for England, but not for Yorkshire.

BRIAN SELLARS, defending Yorkshire's decision to sack Johnny Wardle four days after his selection to join the MCC tour of Australia, **1957**.

What's tha think it is – t' bloody Scarborough Festival?

Park Avenue spectator to John Hampshire, after rapid 42 for Yorkshire v Australians, **1964**.

Don't drift your attention off when you're playing with my money!

RAY ILLINGWORTH to Brian Close during stormy bridge partnership of late **1960s**.

Let him go then, and he can take any other bugger who feels t' same way.

BRIAN SELLARS after Ray Illingworth's 'contract or I'll leave' ultimatum to Yorkshire, **1968**.

Well Brian, you've had a good innings. I'm going to give you the option of resigning or getting the sack.

BRIAN SELLARS, Yorkshire's cricket chairman, to Brian Close, **1970**.

His removal will have to be handled as delicately as a military operation.

Yorkshire committee man, planning removal of Geoffrey Boycott from county captaincy, **1971**.

I could not time the ball. I did what others have done often enough in the past.

JOHN HAMPSHIRE, after infamous Northampton go-slow, **1978**.

They are small-minded people – people who think they are always right. The whole thing was a set-up. They knew they were going to sack me, but at least they could have postponed the meeting. They could have allowed my mother to be buried in peace but they could not wait.

GEOFFREY BOYCOTT to Michael Parkinson, BBC, after sacking as Yorkshire's captain, **1978**.

If they want me to return as captain, they must do something about it. They have got to get together, get off their bottoms and do what they have to do to make it happen.

GEOFFREY BOYCOTT.

It is not for what you have done but because of what you are.

ARTHUR CONNELL, Yorkshire's chairman, informing Geoffrey Boycott why he had lost the county captaincy, **1978**.

It's about time they buried the hatchet – and in the garden, not in one another's backs.

MICHAEL CRAWFORD, Yorkshire chairman, announcing Boycott, Illingworth and Old would remain with club, **1982**.

My lasting memory will be of the greatest of all counties reduced to a squabbling rabble, of squalid, petty argument, of supporters, once the most loyal and sane of all memberships, torn apart by a cult which regarded one man as greater than the club.

JOHN HAMPSHIRE, on feelings as he left Yorkshire for Derbyshire, in *Family Argument*, **1983**.

I don't know of another club in history which finished bottom of the league, sacked its star player and left the manager in the job. The Yorkshire committee are guilty of the biggest whitewash I can ever recall.

BRIAN CLOUGH, on the sacking of Geoffrey Boycott, **1983**.

The decision had to be made – and it should've been made ten years ago.

FRED TRUEMAN, on the same.

When anyone tells me that so-and-so is indispensable, I always reply, 'I know, the churchyard's full of 'em.'

FRED TRUEMAN, defending sacking of Geoffrey Boycott, **1983**.

I am happy and relieved at the outcome. I accept the members' offer to me with joy and humility and will do my best to be worthy of the confidence and affection shown towards me.

GEOFFREY BOYCOTT, reinstalled as a Yorkshire player following members' vote of 'no confidence' in county committee, **1984**.

This decision is a triumph for non-cricketers over cricketers.

SIR LEN HUTTON, after overthrow of Yorkshire committee which attempted to sack Geoffrey Boycott, **1984**.

Geoff has only two points of view. You are either for him or against him. There is no middle ground.

BRIAN CLOSE, resigning as Yorkshire's cricket chairman because he claimed committee was dominated by Geoffrey Boycott, **1984**.

I would like him to resign but I don't think there's an earthly chance of him doing so.

SID FIELDEN, on Geoffrey Boycott's dual role as player and committee man, **1984**.

We are a magnificent and united club and no-one is going to say any different.

REG KIRK, Yorkshire chairman, on day Brian Close resigned as cricket chairman, **1984**.

We are a cricket club not a debating society.

DAVID BAIRSTOW, Yorkshire captain, **1985**.

A dark thundercloud seems to have descended upon this club, clouding the thoughts of those running the club in the day-to-day affairs and affecting the players' team spirit. There are those who have been grabbed by an overriding passion to proliferate their own desires. The situation cannot be allowed to continue. It is destroying what used to be a great cricket club.

VISCOUNT MOUNTGARRET, maiden speech as Yorkshire president at annual meeting in Leeds, **1985**.

One of Yorkshire's faults is that some of the older players live in the part and give the impression that things are no longer as good. Some younger players can't stand talking to them. The game is as good as ever. It's just played under different conditions.

JOHNNY WARDLE, ex-Yorkshire and England left-arm spin bowler, during tragically brief return to county as assistant bowling coach, **1985**.

Surely it is more valid to have a current player among us than whingeing ex-pros.

ROY ICKRINGILL, Harrogate member on Yorkshire committee, defending Geoffrey Boycott's dual role as player and committee man, **1986**.

Most of the things in Yorkshire are not of my own making. People just like to use my name for political reasons.

GEOFFREY BOYCOTT, TV news interview, **1986**.

Ignorant, biased, bigoted, and a bunch of racial idiots.

IAN BOTHAM on the Headingley crowd after the alleged taunting of Viv Richards, **1985**.

Yorkshire followers are very tolerant of ethnic communities. We shall be delighted when the first coloured player arrives in the team.

REG KIRK, then Yorkshire chairman, replying to Botham.

There'll be three or four thousand here. It's not a bad crowd. But ye ken, there's been no charge at the gate. It's a free show.

Scottish local radio man, summing up scene at Perth for Scotland v Yorkshire Benson and Hedges Cup tie, **1984**.

There's no question that being a New Zealander was a bad start in a cricketing sense. We all lacked confidence at birth I guess. We could see the tough way the Australians played and longed to be able to do that, to give them a battle. We were the nice guys.

RICHARD HADLEE, in *At The Double*, **1985**.

I've been surprised at the insolence and the high and mighty attitude of some of the younger Kiwis.

GREG CHAPPELL, **1981**.

Some remarkable incidents marked the progress of the match between New Zealand and New South Wales at Wellington in March, many of the spectators taking exceptions to some of the umpires' decisions. Such conduct was, of course, inexcusable, and would have been so even if it could have been proved beyond doubt that the rulings given had been wrong. The only effect such demonstrations can have is to give a bad name to various centres; they certainly can do no good from the point of view of those who protest. At the close of the match mentioned, the umpires were escorted to the pavilion by three policemen. The matter was regrettable to say the least.

The Cricketer, **1924**.

You wait until New Zealand tour West Indies in 1982. We will get our own back with our umpires.

DERYCK MURRAY, West Indian wicket-keeper, after the controversial Test series in New Zealand, **1980**.

If the West Indies are on top, they're magnificent. If they are down, they grovel. And with the help of Brian Close and a few others, I intend to make them grovel.

TONY GREIG, England captain, before the 1976 series. The West Indies won the series 3–0.

I recommend that future tours to the West Indies should take a good umpire to teach them various laws of the game, of which at the moment the majority are a bit doubtful.

HON. F. S. G. CALTHORPE, MCC captain, tour of West Indies, **1926**.

There's no way at all we should lose. If we do, then a few heads will roll. You could bat for ten days on this pitch and not get a result.

IAN BOTHAM, England's captain, during First Test against West Indies, **1981** (they lost).

When I said that heads would roll, I obviously didn't mean I'd be out there chopping off heads. The media have taken it out of context.

IAN BOTHAM, after England lost the Test by an innings.

Even when they are just spectators, there is something intimidating about their presence.

SIR LEONARD HUTTON, on West Indian cricketers, **1981**.

It is the constant, vigilant, bold and shameless manipulation of players to exclude black players that had so demoralised West Indian teams and exasperated the people.

C. L. R. JAMES, *Beyond A Boundary*, **1963**.

The members were elegant youths of the Pradhu caste and promised very well at first, but their kilted garments interfered with running and they threw the ball when fielding in the same fashion as boarding-school girls. They talked beautiful English, and were perfectly up in English slang, but I was sorry to see their ardour cool.

Report on the formation of the Bombay Union CC, the first Hindu club, in **1866**. Cited by F. S. Ashley-Cooper in *The Cricketer*, 1927, no source given.

You could feel each delivery double declutch on pitching.

COLIN COWDREY on the slow Indian wickets, **1963/4**.

Most responsible Indian officials would admit that the assurance of five full days' gate money was as equally important to them as an interesting finish.

COLIN COWDREY.

Import restriction is so severe that their leading players cannot obtain top quality equipment and if we have achieved nothing else, at least we have furnished their Test players with adequate bats, pads, gloves and boots.

COLIN COWDREY.

It is in the matter of patience that I think the Indian will never be equal to the Englishman.

LORD HARRIS, *A Few Short Runs*, **1921**.

On the Himalayas I have fielded and bowled wearing a mackintosh.

E. H. D. SEWELL on his cricketing days in India in the **1890s**.

We used to have to stop our game at Ooty (Ootacamund) about 4.15 when an enormous bit of coconut matting, 30 yards square, would be laid out over the wickets portion of the ground so that the ponies should not damage that bit.

E. H. D. SEWELL on the annoyance caused by polo to cricketers in India.

A well-captained Parsi, Mohammedan and Hindu side would do better than a mixed one . . . but few Anglo-Indian cricketers could hold out strong hopes of such a side being well-captained.

E. H. D. SEWELL.

Pakistan is the sort of place every man should send his mother-in-law to, for a month, all expenses paid.

IAN BOTHAM on returning from the **1984** tour.

If cricket is regarded, even unconsciously, as an imported game, a freak amusement of an alien race, its roots are shallow.

SIR HILARY BLOOD, on slow progress of cricket in Ceylon, **1955**.

What was once to him an insipid form of recreation is now a new religion and such is his temperament and personality that in years to come he will be an even more faithful patron than his less volatile English counterpart.

PETER POLLOCK, South African quickie, on Afrikaans' growing affection for cricket, **1967**.

I would not have it. They would have expected him to throw boomerangs during the luncheon interval.

CECIL RHODES, explaining why he did not include a coloured player on the South African tour of England which he financed, **1894/5**.

Cricket? It civilizes people and creates good gentlemen. I want everyone to play cricket in Zimbabwe. I want ours to be a nation of gentlemen.

ROBERT MUGABE, Prime Minister of Zimbabwe, **1984**.

To people who kick footballs barefoot and who tread ceremonially on white-hot stones, the impact of a small leather ball at speed is no noteworthy affair.

PHILIP SNOW, founder of Fiji Cricket Association, BBC Radio, **1951**.

The wicket is concrete, the outfield of volcanic ash, and the balls are 'compo'.

Cricket in Ascension Island. Letter to *The Cricketer*, **1927**.

Hurlingham (Buenos Aires) is as fortunate as a town without a saxophone player. The pitch was as flat as an ironing board, and as hard as a landlord's heart.

Buenos Aires Standard on Argentina v MCC, **1927**.

The outlook for Argentina looked as black as a table cloth in a Boca restaurant.

Buenos Aires Standard.

The spectators looked upon the rain with the same friendly feeling that a Bolshevist looks upon a cake of soap.

Buenos Aires Standard.

Where the English language is unspoken there can be no real cricket.

NEVILLE CARDUS.

If the French noblesse had been capable of playing cricket with their peasants, their châteaux would never have been burnt.

G. M. TREVELYAN, *English Social History*, **1944**.

This picturesque view is, to my mind, open to question. It is surely more probable that the combination of Latin temperament and bodyline bowling would have accelerated it (the Revolution).

IAN PEEBLES.

PARIS, 16 APRIL: on Monday last, a cricket match was played by some English Gentlemen in the Champs Elyses (sic). His Grace of Dorset was, as usual, the most distinguished for skill and activity. The French, however, cannot imitate us in such vigorous exertions of the body; so that they rarely enter the lists.

The Times, 1786.

Cricket is the pride and the privilege of the Englishman alone. Into this, his noble and favourite amusement, no other people ever pretended to penetrate: a Frenchman or a German would not know which end of a bat they were to hold; and so fine, so scientific and so elaborate is the skill regarding it, that only a small part of England have as yet acquired a knowledge of it.

REV. JOHN MITFORD, *Gentleman's Magazine*, 1833.

The public in France takes no interest in cricket, of which it does not understand the subtleties, and it sees no fun in 'hitting a ball with a stick'. The Frenchman gets impatient at waiting his turn to go in, and would like to be either batting or bowling the whole time. In a word, cricket is not sympathetic to the French temperament. There are scarcely a dozen Frenchmen who play the game, and most of them play it abominably.

The Times, 1905.

Rangoon cricketers as a class may be termed stay-at-home, so few and far between are visits to or from Burma's neighbours.

'Cricket in Burma', *The Cricketer*, 1928.

The players wear little more than is demanded by the laws of decency, the torrid climate making clothes superfluous, while the pitch is framed in palm-trees.

GEORGE CECIL: 'Cricket in Papua', *The Cricketer*, 1928.

Men, women, boys and girls form the respective elevens. The players' bodies are lavishly smeared with coconut oil, flowers are stuck in the hair, the young girls (some of whom are well favoured) sport tinkling shell earrings, necklaces and bangles. All laugh at hits and misses.

GEORGE CECIL.

It is really remarkable how well the Danes play. Undoubtedly they have the right temperament for the game – denied to the Latin races.

Report in *The Cricketer* on the Incogniti tour of Denmark, **1927**.

In Italy we don't have good net facilities.

ALFONSO JAJERAYAH, captain of the **1985** Italian touring side.

West Indians, that's what we could do with.

JERRY WELLS, a member of the Italian touring team.

I don't believe cricket will become our national sport.

ALFREDO CARDELLI, a member of the Italian touring team.

Altoeliminazione del Battitore che colpisce il wicket.

Italian for 'stumped'.

So far Spaniards have not taken very enthusiastically to cricket.

The Cricketer, 'Notes and Comments' **1921**, on a tour home by English expatriates from Bilbao.

Wicket-keeping has always been a particularly bright feature of American cricket.

G. L. JESSOP.

Not to have experienced the lavish hospitality of our cousins in Philadelphia is to confess to an incomplete cricket career.

G. L. JESSOP.

12
Ladies in Waiting

Players, Wives, Supporters and Others

We've always set the trend. Remember, women cricketers were the first to bowl overarm.

RACHEL HEYHOE-FLINT, requesting women's Test at Lord's during 50th anniversary, **1975**.

Ladies playing cricket – absurd. Just like a man trying to knit.

Anonymous ex-England captain (male) to Brian Johnston.

Sara's fourth ball was quite unlike its predecessors; it had a funny back-break which seemed to puzzle Joan. She cut at it a little uncertainly. It broke again in mid-air and skimmed the off-stump.

The New Girl.

Pitches are like wives, you can never tell how they're going to turn out.

LEN HUTTON, explaining why he put Australia in to bat at Brisbane, MCC tour, **1954/5**.

Last week, at Sileby feast, the women so far forgot themselves as to enter a game of cricket, and by their deportment as well as frequent applications to the tankard, they rendered themselves objects such as no husband, parent or lover could contemplate with any degree of satisfaction.

Nottingham Review, **1833**.

On Thursday week a vast concourse of spectators assembled on the Stoney Fields, Halnaker, to witness a display of the noble game of cricket by eleven married ladies and eleven unmarried from Goodwood, Bogrove and Halnaker. After a fine display the single ladies won, being 45 ahead, having one wicket to go down.

The *Observer*, **1827**.

Professional coaching is a man trying to get you to keep your legs close together when other men had spent a lifetime trying to get them wider apart.

RACHEL HEYHOE-FLINT, former England women's captain.

Some women think that because they play a masculine game they have to look masculine. Some women associated with women's cricket are only ever seen in chunky sweaters and slacks. I get to the stage where I feel embarrassed with some of them.

RACHEL HEYHOE-FLINT.

> I wish you'd speak to Mary, Nurse,
> She's really getting worse and worse.
> Just now when Tommy gave her out
> She cried and then began to pout
> And then she tried to take the ball
> Although she cannot bowl at all.
> And now she's standing on the pitch,
> The miserable little Bitch!

HILAIRE BELLOC, *The Game of Cricket*.

'I think it's simply sickening the way girls want to do everything we do,' said Norris disgustedly.

'Well, she's only thirteen. Seems to me a jolly healthy symptom. Laudable ambition and that sort of thing. Well, I sent some down. She played 'em like a book. Bit inclined to pull, all girls are. So I put in a long hop to the off and she let go at it like Jessop. Smashed my second finger into hash.

P. G. WODEHOUSE, *A Prefect's Uncle*.

Bates is a fool! E's gone and got married id middle o'soomer. 'E should have got married id middle o'winter so that 'e could pay 'is undivided attention to it.

TED PEATE, Yorkshire spinner, on team-mate Billy Bates.

At Tunstall she came to the ground with me every morning and afternoon. I asked her to come there to bat at the nets so that I could practise my spin bowling. Day after day for two solid seasons she helped me in this way, and many's the time she's gone home with her finger nails turned black and blue by blows from my bowling.

CECIL PARKIN on his wife.

Scores of times I have seen her crying with pain through these blows as she stood there patiently holding the bat and trying to defend her wicket against my 'spinners'; but she never gave up.

CECIL PARKIN.

We had cricket for breakfast, dinner and tea. It was like an obsession bordering on madness. He could tell you who scored what years ago – and even what the weather was like. But he could not remember my birthday unless I reminded him.

MILDRED ROWLEY, divorcing her husband, Mike, scorer for Stourbridge CC, **1981**.

Really there is nothing more that I can say. I cannot stop . . . we have got to get on with the game.

MIKE ROWLEY, on tour at the time with Worcestershire Marauders, **1981**.

When we were living in Sydney a friend told me that one night, while she and her husband were making love, she suddenly noticed something sticking in his ear. When she asked him what it was he replied, 'Be quiet! I'm listening to the cricket.'

VICKY RANTZEN, the *Observer*, **1978**.

If the crowd throw bottles at us, we'll hurl 'em straight back –
unless they are full of course.

RACHEL HEYHOE-FLINT, contemplating first England women's tour to West Indies,
1970.

If possible tour with a bachelor team or a side of 'grass-widowers'.

D. L. A. JEPHSON's advice on club tours.

Ten out of eleven women care very little for cricket for cricket's
sake, and though from the goodness of their hearts they insist on
coming to the grounds and sitting through the weary hours till at
length they grow tired, restless, fretful, it would be kinder to all
concerned, and less like cruelty to animals to leave them quietly
at home.

D. L. A. JEPHSON.

There are men who fear women more than they love cricket.

GEOFF SCARGILL, Lancashire annual meeting, proposing women should be allowed
into Old Trafford pavilion, **1985**.

Let them in and the next thing you know the place will be full of
children.

Lancashire member, opposing resolution.

Jeez, Skip, what a piece of glamour. What's that out of ten, Skip?
Five? I know you're a high marker.

GREG MATTHEWS (Australia) to Allan Border, talent-spotting at Headingley during
the **1985** Test. Border did not respond.

On God, if there be cricket in heaven, let there also be rain.

LORD HOME, from *Prayer of a Cricketer's Wife*.

13
Literary Lions

Great Writers on the Great Game

> The Judge to dance his brother serjeant call,
> The Senator at cricket urge the ball.

ALEXANDER POPE, *The Dunciad*, **1742**. The lines are believed to refer to Lord John Sackville.

> England, when once of peace and wealth possessed,
> Began to think frugality a jest;
> So are polite; hence all her well-bred heirs
> Gamesters and Jockeys turned, and Cricket-players.

SOAME JENYNS, political satirist, **1700s**.

> When Death (for Lords must die) your doom shall seal,
> What sculptured Honors shall your tomb reveal?
> Instead of Glory, with a weeping eye,
> Instead of Virtue pointing to the sky,
> Let Bats and Balls th' affronted stone disgrace,
> While Farce stands leering by, with Satyr face,
> Holding, with forty notches mark'd, a board –
> The noble triumph of a noble Lord!

Anonymous pamphlet lampooning the Duke of Dorset, ardent cricketer and Whig politician, **1778**.

Sometimes an unlucky boy will drive his cricket ball full in my face.

DR JOHNSON in *The Rambler*, **1750**.

We were a nest of singing birds. Here we walked, there we played
cricket.

DR JOHNSON on his days at Pembroke College, Oxford.

Cricket. A sport in which contenders drive a ball with sticks in
opposition to each other.

DR JOHNSON, *Dictionary of the English Language*, **1755**.

> Attend all ye Muses, and join to rehearse
> An old English Sport, never praised yet in verse.
> 'Tis Cricket I sing, of illustrious fame,
> No nation e'er boasted so noble a game . . .
>
> When we've played our last game and our fate shall draw
> nigh
> (For the heroes of cricket like others must die)
> Our Bats we'll resign, neither troubled nor vexed,
> And surrender our wickets to those who come next.

REV. REYNELL COTTON, first and last verses of *Hambledon Cricket Song*, **1767**.

> Yet all in public, and in private, strive
> To keep the ball of action still alive,
> And, just to all, when each his ground has run,
> Death tips the wicket, and the game is done.

JAMES LOVE, *The Game Of Cricket* (last 4 lines).

> Hail, Cricket! glorious manly, British Game!
> First of all Sports! be first alike in Fame!

JAMES LOVE, *Cricket: an Heroic Poem*, opening couplet, **1744**.

> That Bill's a foolish fellow;
> He has given me a black eye.
> He does not know how to handle a bat
> Any more than a dog or a cat;
> He has knock'd down the wicket,
> And broke his stumps,
> And runs without shoes to save his pumps.

WILLIAM BLAKE, final stanza of *The Song Of Tilly Lally*.

When all the nations throng the Judgement hill
Where Peter, with his great keys, guards the wicket,
England, in lazy flannels lounging, will
Question the Fisherman: Did you play cricket?

Irish verse.

Of all games or sports, cricket appears to be the most trying to
the temper, for a player cannot lose his wicket without being put
out.

Thomas Hood *circa* **1830**.

Capital game – smart sport – fine exercise – very.

Alfred Jingle in CHARLES DICKENS's *Pickwick Papers*, **1836**.

The scouts were hot and tired; the bowlers were changed and
bowled till their arms ached; but Dumkins and Podder remained
unconquered. Did an elderly gentleman essay to stop the progress
of the ball, it rolled between his legs or slipped between his
fingers. Did a slim gentleman try to catch it, it struck him on the
nose, and bounded pleasantly off with redoubled violence, while
the slim gentleman's eye filled with water, and his form writhed
with anguish. Was it thrown straight up to the wicket, Dumkins
had reached it before the ball. In short, when Dumkins was caught
out and Podder stumped out, All-Muggleton had notched some
fifty-four while the score of the Dingley Dellers was as blank as
their faces.

As above.

Faithful attendant – Quanko Samba – last man left – sun so hot,
bat in blisters, ball scorched brown – five hundred and seventy
runs – rather exhausted – Quanko mustered up last remaining
strength – bowled me out – had a bath, and went out to dinner.

Mr Jingle's account of a single wicket match in the West Indies, Charles Dickens,
Pickwick Papers.

Poor Quanko – never recovered it – bowled on, on my account
– bowled off, on his own – died, sir.

As above.

'But it's more than a game. It's an institution,' said Tom.
'Yes,' said Arthur, 'the birthright of British boys, old and young,
as *habeas corpus* and trial by jury are of British men.'

THOMAS HUGHES, *Tom Brown's Schooldays*, **1857**.

If the wild bowler thinks he bowls,
    Or if the batsman thinks he's bowled,
They know not, poor misguided souls,
    They too shall perish unconsoled.
I am the batsman and the bat,
    I am the bowler and the ball,
The umpire, the pavilion cat,
    The roller, pitch, and stumps, and all.

ANDREW LANG: *Brahma*.

There's a breathless hush in the Close tonight,
Ten to make and the last man in,
And it's not for the sake of a ribboned coat
Or the selfish hope of a season's fame
But his Captain's hand on his shoulder smote:
Play up! Play up! and play the Game!

HENRY NEWBOLT, from *Vitai Lampada*, **1877**.

Now in Maytime to the wicket
    Out I march with bat and pad;
See the son of grief at cricket
    Trying to be glad.

A. E. HOUSMAN: *A Shropshire Lad*, **1896**.

'Cricket', said Raffles, 'like everything else is a good enough sport
until you discover a better . . . What's the satisfaction of taking
a man's wicket when you want his spoons? Still, if you can bowl
a bit your low cunning won't get rusty, and always looking for
the weak spot's just the kind of mental exercise one wants!'

E. W. HORNUNG: *Raffles, The Amateur Cracksman*, **1899**.

Thank God, who made the British Isles
And taught me how to play;
I do not worship crocodiles,
Or bow the knee to clay!
Give me a willow wand and I
With hide and cork and twine,
From century to century
Will gambol round my shrine.

RUDYARD KIPLING, *Cricket Humour*.

Then ye returned to your trinkets;
Then ye contented your souls
With the flanelled fools at the wicket
Or the muddied oafs at the goals.

RUDYARD KIPLING: *The Islanders*, **1902**.

Wake! for the Ruddy Ball has taken flight
That scatters the slow wicket of the Night;
  And the swift batsman of the Dawn has driven
Against the star-spiked Rails a fiery smite.

FRANCIS THOMPSON: *Wake! for the Ruddy Ball has taken flight*.

It is little I repair to the matches of the Southron folk,
Though my own red roses there may blow;
It is little I repair to the matches of the Southron folk,
Though the red roses crest the caps I know.
For the field is full of shades as I near the shadowy coast,
and a ghostly batsman plays to the bowling of a ghost,
And I look through my tears on a soundless-clapping host,
As the run-stealers flicker to and fro, to and fro,
O my Hornby and my Barlow long ago!

FRANCIS THOMPSON, *At Lord's*, **1907**.

'By Hobbs', cried Archie, as be began to put away the porridge,
'I feel as fit as anything this morning. I'm absolutely safe for a
century.'
  'You shouldn't boast with your mouth full,' Myra told her
brother.

A. A. MILNE, 'The Rabbits' in *The Day's Play*, **1910**.

When I said we weren't very good, I only meant we didn't make many runs. Mr Simpson is a noted fast bowler, the Major has an MCC scarf, which can be seen quite easily at point, and I keep wicket. Between us we dismiss many a professor. Just as they are shaping for a cut, you know, they catch sight of the Major's scarf, lose their heads, and give me an easy catch.

A. A. MILNE, 'The Rabbits' in *The Day's Play*, **1910**.

> . . . Walking he rumbled and grumbled,
> Scolding himself and not me;
> One glove was off, and he fumbled,
> Twisting the other hand free.

ARTHUR CONAN DOYLE, *A Reminiscence of Cricket* (stanza 18 of 'The day he bowled W. G. Grace').

> To have been a batsman does not weaken
> The reverence paid to an archdeacon,
> And every bishop knows it biases
> The public favour in his diocese.

ROBERT BRIDGES.

> I see them in foul dug-outs, gnawed by rats,
> And in the ruined trenches, lashed by rain,
> Dreaming of things they did with balls and bats.

SIEGFRIED SASSOON from *The Dreamers*.

Oh, I am so glad you have begun to take an interest in cricket. It is simply a social necessity in England.

P. G. WODEHOUSE, *Piccadilly Jim*, **1918**.

At everything else Chrystal's one of the smartest chaps you ever met, though he does weigh you and me put together, and quite one of the best. But he's so mad keen on cricket that he keeps a pro. for himself and his son of seven, and by practising more than any man in England he scores his ten runs in all matches every season.

E. W. HORNUNG, 'Chrystal's Century' from *Old Offenders and a Few Old Scores*, **1923**.

Once more, most weather-beaten blade,
Old bludgeoner of leather,
We walk before the hushed parade
To face the odds together.

And when your days of battle close,
I'll have your last scars tended,
And on my wall you shall repose,
Triumphantly suspended.

G. D. MARTINEAU, *The Old Bat* (stanzas 1 and 5), **1924**.

I set about consulting the omens for my success in the match. I searched assiduously through the first-class scores, picking out the amateurs whose names, like my own, began with 'S', and whose initial was 'G'. There were only two that day: the result was most unsatisfactory. G. Shaw: run out, 1; G. Smith: c. Lilley, b. Field, 0. According to that I should score half a run. So I called in professional assistance, and was rewarded with Shrewsbury; not out, 127.

SIEGFRIED SASSOON, *Memoirs of a Fox-Hunting Man*, **1928**.

While we were walking across the fields Aunt Evelyn paused on the top of a stile to remark that she felt sure Mr Balfour would be a splendid Prime Minister. But I was meditating about Shrewsbury's innings. How I wished I could bat like him, if only for one day!

SIEGFRIED SASSOON, as above.

(Parson Yalden) enunciated the grace in slightly unparsonic tones, which implied that he was not only Rector of Rotherden but also a full member of MCC and first cousin once removed to Lord Chatwynd.

SIEGFRIED SASSOON, as above.

We considered cricket the most objectionable (of Charterhouse traditions), because it wasted most time in the best part of the year. Nevill suggested a campaign in favour of lawn-tennis. We were not seriously devoted to tennis, but found it our handiest weapon against cricket – the game, we wrote, in which the selfishness of the few did not excuse the boredom of the many.

ROBERT GRAVES, *Goodbye To All That*, 1929.

I well remember . . . at my Big School, after I missed a catch at long-leg, saying to myself 'O Lord, take away my life, for I am not worthy to live!'

JOHN COWPER POWYS, *Autobiography*.

It is that cricket field that, in all the sharp and bitter moments of life as they come to me now, gives me a sense of wholesome proportion: 'At least I am not playing cricket!'

JOHN COWPER POWYS.

A tower we must have, and a clock in the tower,
Looking over the tombs, the tithe barn, the bower;
The inn and the mill, the forge and the hall,
And that loamy sweet level that loves bat and ball.

And now where the confident cuckoo takes flight
Over buttercups kindled in millions last night,
A labourer leans on the stackyard's low wall
With the hens bothering round him, and dreams bat and
ball.

EDMUND BLUNDEN, *The Season Opens* (stanzas 1 and 4).

The sun in the heavens was beaming;
The breeze bore an odour of hay,
My flannels were spotless and gleaming,
My heart was unclouded and gay;
The ladies, all gaily apparelled,
Sit round looking on at the match,
In the tree-tops the dicky-birds carolled,
All was peace till I bungled that catch.

P. G. WODEHOUSE, *Missed!* (first stanza).

Drinking the best tea in the world on an empty cricket ground – that, I think, is the final pleasure left to man.

c. p. snow, *Death Under Sail*, **1932**.

At twelve-thirty, it was decided not to wait for the missing pair, and the nine cricketers started off. At two-thirty, after halts at Catford, the White Hart at Sevenoaks, the Angel at Tunbridge Wells, and three smaller inns at tiny villages, the char-à-banc drew up triumphantly beside the cricket ground of the Kentish village of Fordenden.

a. g. macdonnell, *England, Their England*.

The innings closed at 69, Donald not out nought. Opinion on the gaffers' bench, which corresponded in years and connoisseurship very closely with the Pavilion at Lord's, was sharply divided on the question whether 69 was, or was not, a winning score.

a. g. macdonnell.

GENERAL BURROUGHS: Do you remember Wilmington?
GENERAL FAVERSHAM: Wilmington?
GENERAL BURROUGHS: Fine old service family. Father killed at Inkermann, grandfather blown up under Nelson, an uncle scalped by Indians – oh, splendid record, splendid.
GENERAL FAVERSHAM: What happened?
GENERAL BURROUGHS: Well the general ordered him to gallop through the front lines with a message. Paralysed with funk. Couldn't move. General sent his adjutant, killed before he'd gone 50 yards. Sent his ADC – head blown off. Then he went through with the message himself, lost his arm. Ruined his cricket.

From the film, 'The Four Feathers', **1939**.

CALDICOTT: That German officer looked a lot like old Dickie Randall. You know him, used to bowl slow leg-breaks. He played for the Gentlemen once – caught and bowled for a duck as I remember.
CHARTERS: You think he's a traitor then?
CALDICOTT: But he played for the Gentlemen!
CHARTERS: Ah, but only once.

From the film, 'Night Train to Munich', **1940**.

They vanish, these immortal players, and we suddenly realize with astonishment that years have passed since we heard a passing mention of some of them. At one point they seem as much a part of the permanent scheme of things as the sun which glows upon their familiar faces and attitudes and the grass which makes the background for their portrait; and then, bless us, it is time even for them to go.

EDMUND BLUNDEN, *Cricket Country*, **1944**.

Cricket is a game full of forlorn hopes and sudden dramatic changes of fortune, and its rules are so ill-defined that their interpretation is partly an ethical business. It is not a 20th century game and nearly all modern-minded people dislike it.

GEORGE ORWELL, essay, *Raffles and Miss Blandish*, **1944**.

> Cricket, lovely cricket,
> At Lord's where I saw it;
> They gave the crowd plenty fun;
> Second Test and West Indies won.
> With these two little pals of mine
> Ramadhin and Valentine.

LORD BEGINNER, *Victory Calypso*, **1950**.

It wasn't cricket; it wasn't cricket that an elderly gnome-like individual with a stringy neck and creaking joints should, by dint of head-work and superior cunning, reverse the proverb that youth will be served. It was an ascendancy of brain over brawn, of which, like a true Englishman, I felt supicious.

L. P. HARTLEY, *The Go-Between*, **1953**.

It was a very different half-century from Mr Maudsley's, a triumph of luck, not cunning, for the will, and even the wish to win seemed absent from it. Dimly I felt that the contrast represented something more than the conflict between hall and village. It was that, but it was also the struggle between order and lawlessness, between obedience to tradition and defiance of it, between social stability and revolution, between one attitude to life and another.

L. P. HARTLEY, as above.

SAM: You shouldn't have done that, skipper . . . standing back like that. It was you they wanted to applaud, not me.
JARVIS (*ironically*): You think that's the way it sounded, Sam?
SAM (*gruffly*): Sorry about getting out, anyway.
JARVIS: It doesn't matter, Sam. There's plenty on the board and they can't beat us now.
SAM (*muttering*): All the same, I'd have liked to have given them something to cheer about.
JARVIS: You have, Sam.

Excerpt from 'The Final Test', film starring Jack Warner as Sam Palmer, out for a duck in the Oval Test, **1953**.

Wait a moment, wait a moment. The most extraordinary thing is happening. The whole Australian team is waiting by the wicket and Jarvis is standing back to let Palmer walk into the pavilion alone. And listen to the applause. Listen. (*There is the sound of growing applause, mingled with cheers and shouts of 'Good Old Sam'.*)

(*Voice in a frenzy of excitement*) . . . and they're getting up all round the ground. All round the ground they're standing. This for a man who was out fourth ball. The whole ground – thirty thousand people – standing and cheering – the Australians cheering too – cheering the man they've just dismissed for a duck.

Commentator in the film 'The Final Test', on Sam Palmer's dismissal, **1953**.

> He leaps once more, with eager spring,
> To catch the brief-glimpsed flying ball
> And quickens to its sudden sting:
> The brightness dies: the old eyes fall,
> They see, but do not understand,
> A pursed, rheumatic, useless hand.

JOHN ARLOTT, from *The Old Cricketer*.

> Though wayward Time be changeful as Man's Will
> We have the game, we have the Oval still,
> And still the Gas-Works mark the Gas-Works End
> And still our sun shines and the rain descends.

JOHN MASEFIELD, opening verse of 'Eighty-Five to Win', celebrating England v Australia, The Oval **1882**, from *The Bluebell And Other Verses*, 1961.

At Baron's Lodge there was no suggestion, as there was at, so many schools, that skill at cricket implied moral excellence or that the game itself was a proving ground for life.

SIMON RAVEN, *Close of Play*, **1964**.

For my own sake too I wished that time might stop; that I might stand for ever in the sun, while the trees rustled and the young voices laughed along the terrace, and watch my darling so beautiful and happy at his play. But time slipped on, and my darling started to sweat like a cart-horse, and the Scholars were faced with shameful defeat.

SIMON RAVEN, *Fielding Gray*, **1969**.

> As in life so in death lies a bat of renown
> Slain by a lorry (three ton);
> His innings is over, his bat is laid down:
> To the end a poor judge of a run.

GEORGE MCWILLIAM, Epitaph.

Is there any sex in it?

PETER SELLERS, as psychiatrist, trying to understand cricket, in film 'What's New Pussycat', **1965**.

MOON: Sometimes I dream of revolution, a bloody coup d'état by the second rank – troupes of actors slaughtered by their under-studies, magicians sawn in half by indefatigably smiling glamour girls, cricket teams wiped out by marauding bands of twelfth men.

TOM STOPPARD, 'The Real Inspector Hound', **1968**.

MIRIAM: I don't know if I prefer Rog to have a good innings or a bad one: If it's a good one, he relives it in bed, shot by shot, and if it's a bad one he actually replays the shots until he gets it right. He can make a really good innings last all winter.

From RICHARD HARRIS's play 'Outside Edge'.

While batting once, the Prince of Wales – whose name was
                                        Frederick Louis,
Was hit upon the head, and so his legs went soft and gooey.
He later died because he got that bouncer to the brain,
So in his case you might say the result was 'play stopped
                                        reign'.

RICHARD STILGOE, from song entitled 'The Prince of Wales'.

Index